Books by Margaret Poynter

GOLD RUSH
The Yukon Stampede of 1898
SEARCH & RESCUE
The Team and the Missions

VOYAGER

the Story of a Space Mission

VOYAGER

the Story of a Space Mission

by
Margaret Poynter
and Arthur L. Lane

ILLUSTRATED WITH PHOTOGRAPHS

Atheneum 1984 New York

LIBRARY OF CONGRESS CATALOGING IN PUBLICATION DATA

Poynter, Margaret
Voyager: The Story of a Space Mission

Includes index.
SUMMARY: Discusses the planning, development, and launching of
the Voyager spacecrafts and what happens to the data they transmit to earth.
1. Project Voyager—Juvenile literature.
[1. Project Voyager]   I: Lane, Arthur, joint author.
II: Title.
TL789.8.U6V686   387.8   80-18723
ISBN 0-689-30827-2

Published simultaneously in Canada by
McClelland & Stewart, Ltd.
Manufactured by
Fairfield Graphics, Fairfield, Pennsylvania
Typography by M. M. Ahern
Photo layouts by Marge Zaum
First Printing May 1981
Second Printing February 1983
Third Printing December 1984

To ERIC,
who is made of the right stuff

ACKNOWLEDGMENTS

*I am deeply indebted
to all of those space pioneers
who shared their scientific knowledge
and their excitement
about the Voyager project with me.
My thanks to Charles Stembridge,
Dave Linick, Ray Amorose,
Charley Kohlhase, Dave Durham,
Ron Draper, Fred Scarf,
and Linda Morabito.*

*Thanks also to my husband
who so patiently helped me in ways
that are too numerous to count.*

CONTENTS

INTRODUCTION

SPACE exploration fills a very basic human need—the need to expand our horizons. What if you had been born and raised in a cave? If you didn't eventually leave that limited environment, you'd never feel the refreshing coolness of rain, smell the scent of flowers, or see the vivid colors of a sun-drenched landscape.

However, since you are a human, your natural curiosity would force you to step out of that cave. Perhaps there would be a green valley spread out before you. When you had explored that valley, you would begin to wonder what lay on the other side of the surrounding mountain range. You would climb those mountains.

Man left his cave long ago. He has now explored almost everything on the face of this earth. His explorations enabled him to widen his world—to look at things from different angles. The time has come to extend those explorations to the solar system.

But should we really be exploring other planets when there's so much to be done here on our own planet? Shouldn't we use the money that's being spent on the space program to do more cancer research and to clear up our polluted air?

The answer to these questions is that to explore space *is* to aid in cancer research and to clean up our air. Spinoffs from space technology are now being used in brain surgery, to help people who have heart disease, and in cancer treatment. They are used in pollution control and in waste disposal, in fire prevention, and in protecting the people who fight our fires. Every facet of our lives has benefited from the things that scientists and engineers have learned as they build a spacecraft, and as that vehicle explores the regions beyond our immediate environment. Space programs have helped to improve airline safety and industrial processes, and have aided our law enforcers. They have given us better bridges, farm machinery, and kitchen appliances. The list goes on and will continue to grow.

Eventually, the efforts of space research will teach us ways to convert sunlight into electricity both quickly and economically. More knowledge of our solar system's geology will help us to predict and possibly control earthquakes and volcanic activity. As we better understand the meteorology of other planets, we will better understand the weather patterns of Earth. When we learn more about the development and behavior of living organisms in space, we'll know more about our own biological makeup and our own capabilities.

As we stand back in space, we can gain the new perspective that we need to put our small world in focus. This viewpoint will change our lives for the better. California's governor, Jerry Brown, expressed this thought on the eve of Voyager 1's Jupiter encounter. "As we spend more of our time in space," he declared, "we'll spend less of our time thinking about racial, linguistic, and cultural differences. . . . That's a lot better than war. We'll gain an Earth view instead of a nationalistic view."

This change of viewpoint may be the most important thing to come out of the United States space program. If we turn our backs on this chance to learn, we'll be turning our backs on ourselves. We'll be restricting mankind to one tiny speck called Earth, circling a minor yellow star called the Sun, in an average-sized galaxy. We'll be huddling in a cave, instead of stepping out into a beautiful and spacious valley.

VOYAGER

the Story of a Space Mission

Voyager Science Organizations

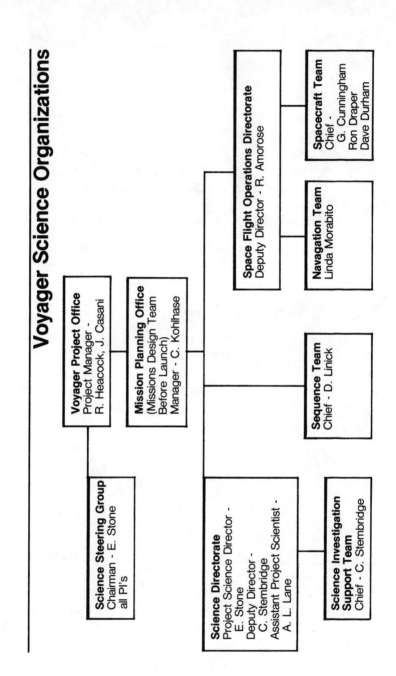

[I]

Cosmic Billiard Balls

"10-9-8-7-6-5-4-3-2-1-0 !" The voice coming over the loudspeaker faded as the rocket engine ignited with a burst of yellow flame. Billowing yellow-white clouds of steam erupted from the water pit that cooled the launch pad, then a thunderous, crackling wave of sound swept over Cape Canaveral. Prodded by the 2.3 million-pound thrust of its Titan-Centaur launch vehicle, the Voyager 2 spacecraft cleared the launch tower and accelerated upward. Twenty scant seconds later it had punctured the bottom of the thin, patchy cloud layer that covered the Cape that morning. Another second passed, and it could no longer be seen from the ground.

While lingering vibrations of sound continued to pulse through the air, a column of smoke connected the launch pad to the overhead cloud layer. A swirling mass

3

of vapor surrounded the launch pad itself. Gently, a breeze started pushing it eastward toward the Atlantic Ocean.

Hundreds of people had gathered on a beach on that morning of August 20, 1977. They were called "bird watchers" by the Cape's permanent residents. There were many tourists in the crowd. To them the event was so spectacular that they would be talking about it for weeks.

A great number of spectators were members of the Voyager team. Some of them had never before seen a launch. The memory of the awesome power of the rocket and the bone-rattling vibrations would stay with them for a long time. Others had seen many previous launches. A few of those veterans might say, "If you've seen one, you've seen 'em all."

Some of the veterans had gone through the agony of seeing a spacecraft dive into the ocean several minutes after lift-off. To them, the launching was a time for a gritting of teeth, a crossing of fingers, and a prayer.

Everyone on the Voyager team had a special feeling on this particular day. They could all look back upon other days and weeks and months of hard work, problems, and frustrations. This launch time was, after all, only one link in a long chain of events that had started ten years earlier. It was the end of one saga, the beginning of another.

*   *   *

THE VOYAGER story began in the middle 1960s when some serious-minded scientists and computer programmers started playing a crazy sounding game. It was called "cosmic billiard balls," or "celestial slingshots." Cosmic billiard balls first became popular at the Jet Propulsion Laboratory (JPL) in Pasadena, California. At this time a JPL advanced planning group was doing some thinking about the next decade of the Space Age. The people in this group were scientists and engineers with imagination and long range vision. They could see what lay ahead in the exciting world of technology. They could look far beyond the upcoming manned landing on the moon, the 1971 orbiters around Mars, and the 1976 Viking landing on that same planet.

Their minds were filled with an idea that almost sounded like science fiction—a Grand Tour of the Outer Planets. They believed that such a journey would be technologically possible in the late 1970s. It was not only possible, but it also *had* to be made at that time. If it weren't, there wouldn't be another chance in their lifetime, or their children's lifetimes.

The deadline existed because of the unique position of the outer planets. In the last half of the 1970s Jupiter, Saturn, Uranus, Neptune, and Pluto would all be aligned in a pinwheel pattern on the same side of the sun. They hadn't had that alignment since George Washington was our president. They wouldn't have it again until the year 2159.

That pinwheel pattern meant that each planet's gravitational pull could be used to speed up the spacecraft, deflect it, and hurl it on to the next planet. In order to use this "gravity assist," or billiard ball effect, the flight path had to be very carefully planned. If the spacecraft came too close to a planet, it would be caught up in its gravity, then either crash or go into an eternal orbit. If it didn't approach the planet closely enough, it wouldn't get the boost that it needed to continue its journey.

Gravity assist, plus a good alignment of the planets, made the Grand Tour more than just a wild dream. But the advanced planning group knew that the Congress of the United States doesn't hand over millions of dollars without some solid proof that a project will work. For instance, what sort of spacecraft would be needed for an outer planets mission? Where would it get its power? All previous spacecraft had used solar cells, which make electrical energy directly from sunlight, because the inner planets are close to the sun. Jupiter is so far away that it gets only one twenty-fifth as much sunlight as does Earth. Saturn gets even less. Solar cells for an outer planet spacecraft would have to be huge in order to collect enough sunlight. They would weigh so much that no existing rocket could launch such a spacecraft to the outer planets.

The solution to that problem came from the nuclear industry. Uranium is used in this industry, and plutonium is a product of uranium reacting with neutrons. When plutonium reacts with oxygen, the resulting compound is plutonium oxide. This compound gives off tremendous heat as it undergoes its natural decay process.

The scientists and engineers who designed the outer planets spacecraft found that plutonium oxide can be processed and condensed and put into a very small, low-weight "package." Its heat can then be conducted into a device called a thermoelectric converter, which changes the heat into electrical energy. In this way a small amount of plutonium oxide can generate enough electrical power —about 450 watts—to run the spacecraft for many years.

The complete energy generating device came to be known as a radioisotope-thermoelectric generator, or RTG. The outer planets vehicle was called an RTG spacecraft. The people who came together to look at the possibilities of this spacecraft formed a group called TOPS, the Thermoelectric Outer Planets Spacecraft study.

The power problem had been solved, but there was another problem to consider. A Grand Tour would take about ten years. How could a spacecraft last that long? Some electrical parts might wear out, so there would have to be plenty of spares. But extra parts would take up room and weight.

The fast growing industry of microintegrated circuitry, which produces pocket calculators, came to the rescue. These tiny circuits could be used to provide all of the necessary backup systems, while taking up very little space and using limited amounts of power.

THE MEMBERS of the TOPS group realized that many of the obstacles to the Grand Tour had been overcome. The spacecraft would have the necessary power. It would have the backup, or redundant, systems to give it a long life. The planets would be lined up in a way in which gravity assist could be used. There were many scientists and engineers who were ready and eager to start the job.

All of the facts worked out by the TOPS team were next thoroughly studied by the Space Science Board (SSB), a group of distinguished scientists. These men and women agreed that the time had come for them to recommend an outer planets mission to the officials at NASA. Such a flight would solve some of the space mysteries that hundreds of years of Earth-based viewing hadn't solved.

As long ago as 1610 Galileo had discovered four of Jupiter's satellites. He named them Io, Europa, Ganymede, and Callisto and wondered how old they were and how they had come into existence. As telescopes were improved, they revealed more details on the surface of Jupiter. Then, in 1654 an Englishman named Robert Hooke saw that planet's Great Red Spot. At first, he thought that this giant blob of color was a high plateau, but later, movement was detected within its borders.

There were also mysterious changes in color. Pink changed to red and orange, then back to pink again. Astronomers asked many questions. What caused these movements and color changes? Is the Great Red Spot an atmospheric storm? If so, why doesn't it die down, as the storms on Earth do?

In the early 1970s, astronomers were still asking many of the same questions as Galileo and Robert Hooke. There were many other mysteries to be solved also. In the 1950s and 1960s large white ovals had been spotted on Jupiter's surface. Where had they come from and why weren't they colored like the Great Red Spot? What is the composition of Saturn's rings? Are they made of rocks or ice?

Does Titan, which is Saturn's largest moon, have an atmosphere? If it does, how dense is it? What kinds of gases does it contain? What is the temperature of Titan's surface?

Through the years, scientists had formed some ideas, or theories, about the things they saw through their telescopes. Some of the theories had been based on facts that had been discovered about the way our own Earth functions. For instance, one idea about the Great Red Spot was that it was very much like the hurricanes with which we are familiar.

Another theory held that the Great Red Spot couldn't be compared to anything on Earth. Perhaps it was a disturbance that was caused by an instability deep in Jupiter's interior. This instability could be caused by internal pressure, which was known to reach millions of pounds per square inch.

There was an idea that the white ovals differed from the Great Red Spot because of a difference in chemicals. There was a theory that Titan's atmosphere was composed of ammonia and methane, and that it caused a "greenhouse effect," which, like a greenhouse's glass, prevents heat from escaping. That effect could hold in the infrared energy and heat up Titan's surface.

The SSB knew the importance of proving or disproving all of these theories. To do so would give scientists a better understanding of the origins and perhaps the future of our own planet. For that basic reason, in 1969 its members recommended a series of five separate missions, the purpose of which was to probe the outer planets. The first would be flown in 1974, and the last in the early 1980s. During these flights, Jupiter would be flown by, probed, and orbited. The other four outer planets would also be investigated, but not quite so thoroughly.

The officials at NASA, the National Aeronautics and Space Administration in Washington, D.C., usually pay close attention to what the members of the SSB recommend. They agreed that the outer planets should be explored. The problem was that they were also thinking about going to Mercury or taking a close look at a comet. The important Viking search for life on Mars had to be continued. There just wasn't enough money to do everything that everyone wanted to do.

There were also some problems with the idea of the Grand Tour itself. Some scientists wondered if it really was the right thing to do. Why go to all five planets? they asked. Why not go just to Jupiter? Maybe we can find out all we want to know there.

Others wondered about the wisdom of sending the expensive RTG spacecraft even to Jupiter. The area is too unknown, they said. How much dangerous radiation is there? And how many large, destructive meteoroids? These people wanted to get more information about what the spacecraft would have to endure.

One big objection to the Grand Tour had to do with the huge amounts of money it would cost. Since it involved so many new kinds of equipment, the estimates were running as high as one billion dollars. That was much, much more than any previous unmanned space project had ever cost.

There were many discussions among the members of the SSB, Congress, and NASA. Many of these discussions turned into arguments. When the tempers cooled down, there were more discussions, then more disagreements. Finally, some compromises were made. The RTG spacecraft would be built, but it would be used in only three flights instead of five. Two of its flights would be made to both Jupiter and Saturn in 1977. A third spacecraft would be built later for a 1979 Jupiter-Uranus mission.

To pave the way for these flights, two much less complicated and less expensive spacecraft would be launched in 1972. These became known as Pioneer 10 and 11. They would take the first close-up pictures and local measurements of Jupiter. Eventually, one of them would be retargeted to fly past Saturn. The information they gathered would be helpful to the engineers who had to build the new RTG spacecraft. They would know, for instance, approximately how much protection from radiation it would need.

In October of 1971 this reduced effort, $350,000,-000 request "package" was sent to Congress along with the rest of NASA's requests for the following year. Now came a time of anxious waiting for all of the men and women who wanted to become part of the outer planets' exploration. President Richard Nixon wouldn't be giving his budget message to the country until the middle of January. Would the new budget include the money for this exploration?

Christopher Columbus must have felt this sort of anxiety as he waited for Queen Isabella's answer to his request for funds. What if she had refused to finance his search for a new route to the Orient? Perhaps he would have found someone else who would give him the money. At least he wouldn't have had to wait 180 years before he could try again.

[2]

The Clock Starts to Tick

INFLATION, unemployment, and the Vietnam War resulted in a lot of bad news in the early part of 1972. To the explorers of space, however, there was one big piece of good news—Congress approved the plan to fly to Jupiter and Saturn in 1977, and the money for the trip was included in the national budget.

The waiting was now over, and it was time to get to work. A project office had to be organized, and people chosen to direct it. Flight plans had to be made, and the construction of the spacecraft started. Three would be built—two for the actual flights, and one to be kept as a spare. There was now an inflexible deadline coming up in 1977, and not a day could be wasted. The clock had begun to tick.

Basically, a space mission starts out like any ordinary journey. Its planners first have to decide what their main destination is, and what side trips they want to take. They have to think about exactly what they want to see, what supplies they'll need, and how much money everything will cost.

The people who were first involved in the outer planets mission knew that they wanted to go to Jupiter and Saturn in 1977, so they called their project MJS77, which is short for Mariner-Jupiter-Saturn, 1977. While they were in the area of each of the planets, they wanted to visit some of their "suburbs," or moons.

Thus, the first big problem they had to think about was what to investigate when they reached each of their destinations. There were so many theories to be proved or disproved, so many questions to be answered. What causes those colorful bands in Jupiter's cloud layers? What are the long, narrow brown blotches that seem to be at the mercy of a very strong wind?

Why does Jupiter make those staticlike radio noises? They seem to occur when the Jovian moon Io is located at a certain place within its orbit. (Jovian, after Jove, another name for the Roman god Jupiter.) Again, why? How? What? When?

Questions, questions, questions. If one of them was answered, ten more sprang up to take its place. All of these puzzles were crying out to be solved, and each one seemed as important as the next. The mission planners at

JPL and NASA headquarters had the big job of figuring out exactly which ones should be investigated during the few hours of the spacecrafts' planetary encounters.

Months passed as scientists and mission planners discussed various possible investigations. Their opinions often collided head-on, and entire meetings were spent in making compromises or discarding ideas. Finally, everyone agreed on a list of tasks for the spacecraft to do. Many of them involved the study of unexplored interplanetary space. These investigations would reveal important facts about the relationship between the sun and the planets. It was already known that the sun is constantly bombarding space with streams of electrically charged particles. Scientists wanted to know exactly what happens when this "solar wind" runs into a solid body or into a planet's magnetic field. They would then know much more about how the sun affects our own atmosphere and interacts with our magnetic field.

Now that the spacecrafts' work had been laid out, the mission planners had to think about what kinds of scientific instruments could be used to do that work. They knew that they would have to have a radio system for transmitting and receiving information. That system could also be used to answer some science questions. Two television cameras would form the spacecraft's imaging system. They would take the first high resolution, close-up pictures of the outer planets and their satellites. How exciting it would be to see if Callisto really did have "ice volcanoes," areas where water has oozed out of the crust and formed huge, frozen waves.

The imaging and radio systems would be very complex. Since they had to be tied into the spacecraft at many different points, their construction was to be managed by JPL engineers. During each step of assembly, they would be tested to see how they interacted with the spacecraft. An imaging team, composed of both engineers and scientists, had to be formed to manage the camera system, and a radio science team would manage the radio system's scientific activities.

The NASA mission planners had to find the people for these teams. They also had to find the people who would both build and manage the other scientific instruments on the spacecraft. To let as many scientists and engineers as possible know about the MJS77 mission, 10,000 Announcements of Flight Opportunity were sent out all over the world. They were received, read, and discussed in the foyers of embassies, in the classrooms of universities, and at the meetings of scientific organizations.

Many people were excited about the possibility of exploring the outer planets. Some of them were already working on instruments that they thought would be useful for such a mission. They started telephoning and writing letters to contact other people who might be interested in forming a team. There was a deadline for responding to the Announcement, so they couldn't waste any time.

* * *

AT THIS TIME a physicist named Fred Scarf had still not recovered from the disappointment of being turned down for the earlier Pioneer mission to Jupiter. For many years he had wanted to study plasma waves, which are movements within clouds of ionized gas. These clouds are often formed by charged particles that come from the sun or from planetary atmospheres. When the sun's charged particles mingle with the Earth's atmosphere, strange things occur. Some of these things had been investigated by Earth-orbiting spacecraft, but the rest of the answers lay in interplanetary space. Fred couldn't understand why NASA hadn't included a plasma wave instrument on Pioneer. When there was talk about doing the Grand Tour, Fred started hoping again. He felt that some of his answers would be found at Jupiter. As soon as he saw the Announcement of Flight Opportunity for the MJS77 mission he made some telephone calls to other people who had tried to get a plasma wave investigation on Pioneer. He spoke to scientists at the University of Minnesota, and at Stanford, the University of California at Los Angeles, and JPL. He also called Don Gurnett at the University of Iowa. Everyone agreed to work on a mutual proposal, a long report in which they would describe the kind of instrument they could build, what the instrument could accomplish, and why they were the people who should be selected for the project. Meanwhile, other groups of scientists at other universities were also writing plasma wave proposals as well as proposals for all sorts of other investigations.

Fred Scarf and the people in his group were certain that one of the plasma wave proposals would be accepted this time. So were all the other men and women who were writing such proposals. After all, it didn't seem likely that the officials at NASA Headquarters would send up *another* Jupiter spacecraft without this important investigation on board.

[3]

"NASA regrets to inform you . . . . "

W AITING is never easy. For Fred Scarf and all of the others who were eager to become a part of the MJS mission it was especially difficult. This exploration might enable them to gain information that would open up new horizons, not only for themselves, but for scientists all over the world.

The long months of the reviewing process wasn't easy for the people who had to judge the proposals either. Over fifty people had responded with proposals to be on the imaging team alone. Most of them had the highest of qualifications, but only about fifteen could be chosen. The situation with the radio science team was almost as overwhelming. On top of that, there were one hundred teams who had proposed other investigations, many of them with instruments they would supply to the spacecraft. Only a handful of them would be receiving the prized telegrams of congratulations.

As the reviewers sorted through the proposals, they had to keep many questions in their minds. Can this instrument really do the things it's supposed to do? Will it measure what it's supposed to measure? Will it be too expensive for our budget? Can it fit into the space and weight limitations of the spacecraft? How much data will it produce? And how much power will it use? Can it be built using present day tools and technology?

Those engineering questions were usually rather easy to answer. They all had to do with pounds and dollars and other things that could be measured. There were other factors that were much harder to decide upon, because they were intangible. They couldn't be handled, or weighed, or fed into a computer. What kinds of people are on this team? Do they have the right blend of experience and skills? Will they be able not only to collect the right data, but to analyze and organize it so that other people can make use of it?

And do these people have their feet planted solidly on the ground? The men and women who fly a space mission must have a lot of imagination, but their work has to be based on nothing but cold, hard facts.

When the reviewers thought they had the right answers to all of those questions, they graded each of the proposals. Finally, they had gone through all of them and rated them from the best choices down to the ones that they considered unworkable, or unimportant to the purpose of the mission. More time passed as NASA officials looked over these ratings. The review process ended when they put their stamp of approval on the winners.

A few of the winners weren't entirely pleased with the final decisions. Some of the people they had wanted to be on their team had been left out, and new ones substituted. These forced partnerships had occurred because the officials at NASA had thought a particular team needed more balance between people with various types of abilities. Some of these partnerships worked out well. Some didn't. When a group of men and women have to work together for years under a lot of pressure, conflicts can break out even among the best of friends. When those people don't know each other, or don't get along too well to start with, the conflicts can develop into serious problems. If the problems remain unsolved, they may eventually interfere with the smooth working of the mission. A space project depends as much on human cooperation as it does on nuts, bolts, and scientific know-how.

The people who had been chosen for the mission had good cause to celebrate. Not so for Fred Scarf, Don Gurnett, and their colleagues. Instead of a congratulatory telegram, they received another letter from NASA. "I regret to inform you . . ." were the ominous words at the top of the page.

* * *

THE PRINCIPAL Investigators (PI's), the men who had been selected to lead the teams, lived and worked in such widely separated locations as Maryland, Arizona, Colorado, and Massachusetts. The members of their teams came from as far away as France and England. There were planetary astronomers, meteorologists, and geologists. There were theoreticians and mathematicians. There were also people who were "hardware oriented." They were the ones who took ideas and turned them into a scientific instrument.

The winning instruments fell into three separate groups. One group—the optical instruments—are located on each spacecraft's scan platform. They have very narrow fields of view, so they have to be pointed accurately at their targets. From those targets they collect radiant energy (light, for instance) to create and form images, or "spectra," or sometimes both. The spectral lines are obtained by passing light through atmospheric gas. Each type of gas has its own characteristic spectral lines. By looking at these data, scientists can understand the physical and chemical characteristics of the planets, their satellites, and some aspects of interplanetary space.

The second group consists of four instruments that sense and measure various aspects of the interplanetary environment. One collects certain data on solar plasma. Another measures low-energy charged particles, and a third, high-energy cosmic rays. The fourth, a magnetometer, which measures magnetic fields, has several parts spread out along a fifty-foot boom. All of these instruments have a wide viewing range.

By studying the data this group of instruments collects, scientists can better understand the relationships between the sun and the planets, and the interactions of a planet and its moons.

The last group consists of the radio astronomy and the radio communications systems. By passing radio waves through a planet's atmosphere, scientists can learn many facts about its physical nature and structure.

All of these instruments were in the process of being built when Pioneer 10 reached Jupiter. Based on the information it sent back, some of the officials at NASA began to wonder whether or not they had made a mistake in not selecting Fred Scarf's plasma wave investigation. Fred heard about their doubts and asked many of his well-known friends to write letters in support of his ideas. Jim Warwick, who had been selected to head up the planetary radio astronomy investigation, got everyone on his team to write and call NASA headquarters about the plasma study. The officials there were impressed by the enthusiasm for Fred and his proposed investigation.

On July 4, 1974, Fred received an invitation to a NASA meeting. Don't get your hopes up, he kept telling himself as he flew to Washington, D.C.

When Fred Scarf left that meeting, he felt as if he

were ten feet tall. His plasma wave investigation was going to be flying on the MJS77 mission! He could hardly wait to get to work.

But two more long weeks passed before he could start. Don Gurnett was in Arizona, taking part in a sailplane competition. Since he was in the finals, he couldn't tear himself away from the exciting event.

Fortunately, the plasma wave instrument is a small, uncomplicated device, and Jim Warwick offered to let Fred share his antennas. Thus, although he was starting late, Fred knew he could finish in time for the long testing period before launch.

At that moment his biggest worry was getting enough viewing time during encounter. He felt that his investigation was still considered a sort of "second cousin" to the others. At one point he was to be allowed only one forty-eight-second block of time. He needed much more.

Still, Fred thought, any time my team gets is better than not having my instrument on the spacecraft at all.

[4]

Plenty of Headaches

WHILE Fred and his fellow scientists were fashioning their scientific instruments, a group of JPL engineers was working on the spacecraft that would transport those instruments. The building of any spacecraft is a tricky job that involves a lot of pressure and attention to detail. When the finished product is put onto the launch pad, it has to be as close to perfection as anything man can make when there is a limited amount of dollars and of time. During its explorations, it may endure such hazards as being baked by solar heat, bombarded by electrically charged particles, and caught up in a radiation field a thousand times more powerful than any that occurs near the earth. While undergoing these ordeals, the spacecraft is expected to keep right on with its job of gathering and transmitting information.

The two MJA spacecraft were going to have to face

more unknown obstacles than any spacecraft that had ever been flown. Pioneer 10 and 11 had revealed a few of the dangers that lay in wait. Beyond that sketchy information, scientists could only guess about many of the conditions in Jupiter's environment. What would happen when a spacecraft entered the planet's magnetosphere? Exactly how much radiation would it have to absorb?

Their thoughts about Saturn were based upon even less factual knowledge. Even if one of the Pioneers made it to that planet, the information it sent back wouldn't be available until long after the MJS spacecraft had been launched.

It was known that there is a belt of asteroids and micrometeoroids between Mars and Jupiter. In 1972, no one knew exactly how wide that belt was, nor how dense. Were the small particles far enough apart to allow a spacecraft to slip through unharmed? And how many larger particles were there? A marble sized rock, if it's traveling fast enough, can put a big hole through the fragile body of a spacecraft.

As with every space vehicle, each nut, bolt, seal, and hinge had to be tested and retested. The MJS spacecraft had several systems that not only had to be tested, but developed from scratch. Thus, there were plenty of questions to be answered before anyone could even pick up a riveting gun or a welding torch. Blueprints, plans, and designs were drawn and discussed at endless meetings. A lot of ideas that looked good on paper had to be scrapped because they would never work out in reality. This one looks great, everyone might agree, but won't it make the spacecraft overweight? We sure can't use this other one because it wouldn't fit under the nose cone of the rocket. This third one doesn't have the right balance. The attitude control thrusters would have to work overtime to keep the spacecraft facing in the right direction. Maybe we could move this over here and that over there. . . .

No, we can't do that. The radiation coming from the RTG's would destroy it in less than a year. Shouldn't we do this, or that, or examine another possibility?

As the planning progressed, the precious time was slipping away. The two spacecraft had to be completed a year before launch. It would take that long for the engineers to make the final checks and tests and to follow them up with emergency repairs and minor design changes.

Time wasn't the only thing that put pressure on the Spacecraft Design Team. Money was another. Congress had allotted only a certain number of dollars to do the job. There couldn't be any expensive mistakes, and the waste had to be kept as low as was humanly possible.

More time passed, and more money was spent before the design team was ready to build a mock-up—a full scale model of the spacecraft. By that time, the engineers knew exactly where the scientific instruments were to be placed, and how much of the spacecraft's 450 watts of power they would draw. They knew how much fuel the spacecraft would need and where it should be stored. They had designed special compartments for the onboard computer and the tape recorder, and had shielded the more delicate parts from the possibility of radiation damage. They hoped that their radiation testing had given them a good enough idea of just how much protection was needed.

Many of the systems and parts were being designed, constructed, and tested by various companies all over the United States. As they arrived at JPL, they were installed on the mock-up and tested again. The engineers had to know how the moving parts would behave in a vacuum, and in extreme heat and cold.

Will those parts perform not just a few hundred times without a "hiccup," but hundreds of thousands of times? One small part—the valve that controls the release of the liquid fuel into the thrusters—had to be reliable enough to perform *millions* of times without hesitation, and not stick in the opened or closed position. Some samples of these valves were put into a vacuum tank. For months they were forced to operate every few fractions of a second. Unless they were perfect enough to stand up under that exhaustive test, the spacecraft wouldn't fly.

Added to the time and money problems was the problem of weight. No human dieter ever watched the scales more carefully than the design team watched the mounting weight of its vehicle. Each fully loaded MJS spacecraft could weigh no more than about 1,800 pounds, and fifty of those pounds would be taken up by radiation shielding. On the wall of the project office there was a big tote board upon which the daily mounting poundage was tallied. The antenna, the booms, the scan platform, the cameras—everything had a maximum weight allowance assigned to it. The JPL people had to try to come in *below* their allowance. Most of them knew from experience that at least one or two of the science instruments would come in *over* their allotted weight.

To stay within the weight limitation, and to insure the spacecraft a long life, the design engineers decided to use a new type of attitude control system. The one they chose had been going through experimental development for several years. It uses a liquid gas called "hydrazine," instead of the compressed nitrogen gas that was used on the earlier Mariner and Viking spacecraft.

When a single droplet of hydrazine reaches one of Voyager's sixteen minithrusters, the liquid reacts with a metal inside the thruster. At that time, several gases are produced. They expand and spurt out of the thruster's nozzle at a very high speed.

When several of the thrusters are "burned" at once, the combination of the spurts is forceful enough to turn and twist the spacecraft into a new attitude, or orientation in space. It would take several such "burns" of compressed gas to result in the same force. Thus, one pound of hydrazine is equal to about one hundred pounds of compressed nitrogen gas.

Aside from being so economical in weight, hydrazine can be used for both attitude control and also for the major course corrections that must be made occasionally. As a result, there's no necessity to have the extra compressed gas system that used to be used for attitude control. Altogether, the use of hydrazine saves about 200 pounds of weight.

Time, money, weight. As if that combination weren't enough to worry about, the MJS spacecraft had to be super-reliable. Instead of the two or three years that an inner planet spacecraft had to function, this outer planet vehicle had to last eight years. Its designers were always on the lookout for materials that were both light-weight and durable. They felt fortunate to find a new glass-reinforced graphite that weighs about one tenth as much as steel, and that expands and contracts very little during temperature changes. This characteristic means that there is a minimum amount of wear and tear on hinges and other moving parts.

IN JANUARY of 1976, the United States Congress added another problem to the ones that the spacecraft team already had. NASA's request for money to send a separate flight to Uranus in 1979 was turned down. The MJS project officials had half-expected this refusal and had made some plans to get around it. They would first wait and see if the first spacecraft to arrive at Saturn had a good encounter with the planet and Titan, its largest moon. If it did they would alter the trajectory for the second spacecraft and fly it to Uranus after its Saturn encounter.

Going to Uranus involved much more than just changing a trajectory, however. Such an encounter required a very sensitive infrared spectrometer, an instrument that measures a planet's temperature and the materials in its atmosphere, among other things. Many scientists thought that the spectrometer that was being built for the Jupiter and Saturn encounters wouldn't be good enough at Uranus. Six million dollars was poured into a crash program to develop a better instrument. The company that was given the job should have been allowed four years to complete it. Instead, it was allowed only eighteen months.

Nevertheless, as those months drew to a close, it looked as if the improved spectrometer would be flying on the spacecraft. Computer programs were designed for it, and engineers drilled new bolt holes and installed new interface cables on the spacecraft. To be on the safe side, however, they also installed the first instrument—the one that had been designed for Jupiter and Saturn only.

It's a good thing they did, because just before launch time, the new spectrometer failed a final vibration test. It was disappointing to come so close, and then not succeed.

Still, everyone thought philosophically, it had been worth the try.

ANOTHER, more serious, problem occurred during the attempts to design the radio system for the spacecraft. This radio system works on two frequencies—the S-band and the X-band. The S-band is used to send back low-rate, ordinary, everyday engineering information, such as whether or not the thrusters are doing their job of keeping the spacecraft stable and on course, how much fuel is left, and what the temperature is on various parts of the spacecraft. It's also used during the cruise phases between the planets for occasional science investigations. The S-band data stream is relatively slow, but its message comes in loud and clear over great distances, and even through bad weather in Earth's atmosphere.

The higher frequency X-band is used during the busy encounter times when the science instruments are measuring, observing, and gathering information as fast as they can. It's capable of transmitting fifty to one hundred times more data than the S-band can in the same length of time. At Jupiter, for instance, the X-band was able to keep up with the imaging system, which was designed to take a picture every forty-eight seconds. The S-band would have been able to send back only one picture every ten minutes, so most of them would have been lost.

The problem arose because the X-band signal

would be very weak if Voyager used the low-power transmitter that had been used on earlier space missions. It would be almost useless at far-off Uranus. A way had to be found to "beef it up," so the JPL engineers decided to use a more powerful transmitter. The hitch came when they tried to find a tube for that transmitter. None existed, so it had to be designed and built. The contract for the work was given to a company that specializes in this type of product.

Since the tubes had to be made in a very special, very exacting way, the process at best was going to be slow and tedious. The parts had to be machined to a very fine tolerance, baked in just the right way, then cooled slowly, and carefully assembled.

Starting with the first attempt, nothing worked right. The machinists had a lot of trouble producing the parts that made up the inside of the tube. Later, when the glass jackets were put over the tube, the ceramic-to-metal seals leaked. Next, a batch of the metal that had been used was found to have impurities in it. The problems kept appearing, and time and money were running out.

A year before launch, when the spacecraft should have been completed and ready for its final testing, the tubes still weren't ready. The project officials began to realize that they might have to fly the mission without the high-power X-band transmitter. Several people at NASA Headquarters agreed with that gloomy prediction.

The order from NASA came down. "Get to work

and find out what we can accomplish with these two spacecraft if we don't have that new transmitter."

Charley Kohlhase, the Mission Design Manager, and Lonne Lane, the Assistant Project Scientist, joined three other people in an attempt to salvage what they could from the project if they didn't have the high power X-band. For five days they worked from early in the morning until well after midnight. To save time they ate quick meals at nearby restaurants and rarely went home. Hour after hour they studied the scientific measurements and every major observation that had been planned for each of the three planetary encounters.

Which information is the most important? they asked themselves. Which views of each satellite can we leave out of our investigations? Maybe we can leave the pictures out in this two-hour period. And what about moving this measurement up to the next hour? That way we can observe the Great Red Spot and still do these other things. But then what will happen to the next set of measurements? Maybe we can put some of the data on the tape recorder and transmit it to Earth later.

When the crash study was over, they reported their findings to the Project Manager. The situation at Jupiter wouldn't be too bad without the high-power X-band transmitter. There would be some serious problems during the Saturn encounter. And at Uranus the lack of that transmitting tube would be disastrous for the optical instruments.

Just when everyone had resigned themselves to limping along without the new transmitter, the contracting company came up with six tubes that looked as if they might do the job. Out of the six, two were picked for each spacecraft. Some quick testing was done, and they were installed.

No one was very optimistic that those tubes would keep on working for eight years. The spacecraft engineers had hoped that they would be able to pick the best out of a choice of fifty good ones. Instead, they had had to pick from only half a dozen, and there was not time to test them thoroughly. At launch time they knew that all they could do now was to hope.

THE PEOPLE in charge of building the MJS spacecraft took plenty of headaches home with them every night. Those problems plagued them as they ate dinner, watched television, and went shopping. The tape recorder failed today. Where can we get a tape that won't stick? Do we have enough radiation shielding on the spacecraft? But what if we don't? We can't afford to put on any more weight.

We're spending money much too fast. Will our budget hold out? And the photopolarimeter team needs help. Who can we spare to go to Colorado? Or who can we send to Maryland to help with a new power supply design for their instrument? Can't let any of those investigator teams go under. What good would the spacecraft be without its science payload?

A week never passed without the appearance of new problems, or the worsening of old ones. Sometimes it seemed as if the whole project should never have been started in the first place.

Was it possible that man wasn't supposed to know what lay in the dark reaches of the outer solar system?

[5]

An Outer Planetary Travel Agency

IMAGINE, for a moment, that you own a travel agency. A group of tourists wants to charter a bus to go to a distant city, and you're in charge of planning the trip. There's a choice of several possible routes, all of which contain hazards, such as rough roads, mountain ranges, and possible stormy weather. None of them has a gas station or a garage along the way. Will you run out of fuel? Will the bus break down? Can you transport your passengers in comfort and safety?

Your problems won't be over when you arrive at your destination. You can spend only one day in the city, and the bus will be your only transportation. Every person in the group wants to do something different. One of them is going to a museum; another to the zoo, and a third to a bowling alley. One of the women has made plans to visit her sister who lives in the suburbs. How can you be in all of those places at one time?

It's obvious that this trip is going to have to be planned very carefully. First, you'll want to make sure that you have some spare parts for your bus, such as an extra tire, fan belt and radiator hose. Arrange a meeting with all of your passengers and tell them that each of them can spend only a certain amount of time doing what he wants. When that time is up, the bus will have to move on to something else. Everyone will have to make a sacrifice, so that all will have a fair share of the limited time.

This imaginary bus tour is a lot like a real space flight. There are thousands of problems to be solved before the spacecraft leaves the ground. Which flight path, or trajectory, is the safest and will use the least fuel? Which one will result in gaining the most scientific information? How can the spacecraft be kept alive until it finishes its job? It's going to need a lot of backup systems and parts. How can all of them be installed without making it overweight?

The problems don't disappear when the spacecraft arrives at its target planet. So far, no spacecraft has carried any hard-to-please tourists, but they do carry scientific instruments. And behind each of these instruments are many people who have spent years preparing for the mission. It's easy to understand how eager they are to get as much information as they can during the limited encounter time.

No science team ever gets as much viewing time as it wants. The instruments have to take turns using the spacecraft's limited power. They all have to share the communications link back to earth. A scan platform can be turned in only one direction at a time. If there are three or four exciting events going on at one time, which one should be observed?

What happens when there's some sort of failure or emergency and some of the observations or series of pictures have to be left out? Which ones should be discarded? Of course, the answer is the least important ones. But which *are* the least important? For anyone who's flying an instrument on a spacecraft that can be an almost impossible decision to make. Someone else will have to do it, and that's part of the job of the mission design team. Its members are the "tour directors" of a space mission.

The MJS Mission Design Team was made up of about a dozen specialists who represented various parts of the project. At launch time, the Mission Design Team became the Mission Planning Office. Its job remained basically the same—to lay the long-range plans, to see that everyone had the necessary supplies to do the job, to scout ahead for trouble, and to prepare for and, if possible, avoid emergency situations.

At any one meeting of the Mission Design Team

there might have been an expert on computers, another on the spacecraft's power system, and a science investigator who spoke for the eleven Principal Investigators. Sometimes a representative from the Deep Space Tracking Network (DSN) attended a meeting. He helped to schedule the big radio antennas in Australia, Spain, and California. These antennas track spacecraft and receive the data they transmit. At any one time, there may be two or more spacecraft flying, but an antenna can track only one at a time. If there is more than one spacecraft over a tracking area, the tracking time has to be split up between them. The one that is returning the most valuable information will get the lion's share of that time.

The MJS Mission Design Team was well aware that there might be tracking conflicts with either the Pioneer or the Viking spacecraft.

THE LEADER of a mission design team is usually a "generalist." That's a person who once specialized in a particular field, but whose interests led him off into other fields also. He knows enough about each aspect of the project to ask pertinent questions, to understand the answers, to give helpful suggestions, and to help set up mission policies. He uses his specialized knowledge on many of the problems that occur.

The MJS Mission Design Team was fortunate to have Charley Kohlhase as its leader. Using his unique talents, Charley was able to pull everything and everyone together into a smoothly working unit. Every day he had to tie dozens of details from one part of the project to another. All of these connecting links were important, and Charley had to keep track of each one over a period of several years. He knew the limitations of the spacecraft and of the ground-based equipment. A big part of his job consisted of making sure that the spacecraft got the most science return while working within those limitations.

He not only had to keep track of what was happening, but what *might* happen. What if a computer at JPL were to "crash" during an encounter time? There has to be a "hot backup" computer programmed and ready to go at the flick of a switch. What if there's a storm over a DSN station when one of the spacecraft is transmitting some important information? The X-band is very "weather sensitive." If there's much dampness or rain in the air, its signal may be absorbed and not reach the ground receiving antenna. At those times the spacecraft may have to be ordered to lower its data rate so there will be more power in the signal.

In this case, some of the previously planned pictures and measurements will have to be left out. Again, which ones are the most valuable? If the Mission Design Team and the scientists have made these decisions ahead of time, the situation is a lot easier to handle.

What if one of the worst possible things had happened, and one of the spacecraft had blown up on the launch pad? That would have been a real catastrophe, but how much worse it would have been without an alternate plan. The Mission Design Team had prepared one in which the remaining spacecraft would perform double duty.

ONE OF the first things that the Mission Design Team had to do was to pick out two trajectories, one for each spacecraft. These flight paths had to be based on the scientific goals of the mission. One spacecraft was to have a close encounter with Jupiter and Io, and take more distant looks at four other Jovian satellites. It was then to go on to Saturn for a close look at the large satellite Titan. The other spacecraft's Jupiter encounter wasn't to be as close, and it was to view different "faces" of the satellites than its sister ship had seen.

No one really knew whether or not the first spacecraft would make it through Jupiter's powerful radiation field. If it were destroyed, the other one, by avoiding most of the radiation, would be able to complete the mission. In any event, it would go on to Saturn, and then possibly to Uranus.

Going to the outer planets isn't quite the same as going to London, or to Peking. Obviously, the distance is much greater. There's also the fact that cities stay put, while planets and satellites are always on the move. The people who design space missions have to know not only exactly where their targets are at launch time, but where they will be on the desired arrival date.

Planning an encounter with only one planet is a complicated enough affair. The MJS people had to consider the present and future positions of three planets and a dozen satellites. Fortunately, these celestial bodies have their own schedules, and they unfailingly stick to them.

After "roughing out" many possible flight paths on a computer, the Mission Design Team found that the best "launch window" would be a thirty-day period spanning August and September of 1977. Depending upon which of those thirty days was chosen, and upon the angle and length of the particular trajectory, the spacecraft could arrive at Saturn on any one of 400 days, from November, 1980, to December, 1981. Multiply thirty by 400. You'll find, as did the MJS people, that they had to pick the best two trajectories from *12,000* possibilities.

To start this huge task, the team members first eliminated the trajectories that had the worst problems. For instance, no one wanted a spacecraft to arrive at a planet when the sun was between that planet and Earth. If it did, the sun's radio noise would completely block out the spacecraft's radio signal. Consequence? There would be no radio communication between the spacecraft and Earth, and thus no data or pictures from that encounter.

Where will the planet's satellites be located on any particular encounter date? If Io was on the opposite side of Jupiter when the spacecraft arrived, the cameras wouldn't be able to take close-up pictures. Titan circles

Saturn once every sixteen days. It's in a good position for a spacecraft to take high resolution pictures of it on only one out of those sixteen days. Where will the satellites or the planet be in relation to the sun on any one day? Sunlight is essential for taking clear photographs.

How close to the planet will the spacecraft get with this trajectory or with that one? It has to be close enough to make observations, but not so close that gravity will cause it to crash, or to change its flight path too much. Which side of the planet will the cameras be seeing on this trajectory? Is that the most interesting side? But how do we know which side *is* the most interesting?

And most important, will this trajectory use more fuel than the spacecraft is capable of carrying?

Hundreds and hundreds of questions were asked, then answered as the weeks and months passed. Slowly, the number of trajectories was whittled down. When two years had passed, there were only ninety-eight possibilities left. These were recorded on computer tape and loaded into the Titan-Centaur launch vehicles. As time passed, circumstances weeded out all but ten of those ninety-eight possibilities. Finally, it appeared that August 20 and September 1 would be the most ideal launch dates. The sense of urgency grew sharper as everyone on the project targeted his efforts toward those two days.

THE MJS MISSION Design Team also had to plan a general itinerary, a sort of traveler's guide book, for the journey of the two spacecraft. This "mission profile" was divided into phases—Launch, Near Earth, Far Earth, Earth-Jupiter Cruise, Jupiter Encounter, Jupiter-Saturn Cruise, Saturn Encounter, and Post-Saturn Encounter. All of the major scientific and engineering events were fitted into these various phases. The first four phases were filled in with great detail before launch time.

At lift-off each spacecraft's computer had been supplied with hundreds of instructions. Some of these were basic engineering commands, which would be used again and again during the course of the flight. Others told the spacecraft what to do and what to expect during the first few hours of its journey. When those instructions had been used up, more were transmitted, or "uplinked," from Earth for the next part of the trip.

Since a computer can hold only a certain number of instructions at one time, this uplinking process continues throughout the scientific life of the spacecraft. These complex robots never outgrow their need for the guiding hand of man.

By launch time the two spacecraft had been officially named Voyager 1 and Voyager 2. The first one launched would have a later arrival date at Jupiter and Saturn than the second one launched. Thus, it was Voyager 2 that lifted off on August 20, 1977.

Only minutes after that lift-off, man was going to have to come to its rescue.

The launch vehicle just before lift-off. The two white rockets at the bottom contain the Titan solid rocket motors. The Titan core with its two stages is situated between the rockets. The top of the vehicle is the Centaur rocket. The spacecraft is located inside the Centaur, just below the white shroud at the top.

It took ten years of planning, studying, testing and building, but at last the Voyager spacecraft was ready to start its journey. The circular object at the top is the high-gain antenna. It is mounted on the spacecraft "bus," which houses the electronics. The white slats on the bus are thermal louvers. The wrapped object just below the bus is the propulsion module. It provides the final kick out of Earth's orbit and into the Jupiter trajectory.

Ray Heacock, Voyager Project manager, and Glenn Cunningham, chief of the Spacecraft Team, go over a model of the Voyager spacecraft.
TERRY ANDRUES

*Charley Kohlhase
presents an idea during
an SSG meeting.*
TERRY ANDRUES

*Lonne Lane, Assistant
Project Scientist and
co-author of this book,
has seen the Voyager
mission through many
emergencies.*
TERRY ANDRUES

*This diagram of the
Voyager 2 encounter
trajectory shows the
point of closest approach
(periapsis). The Sun
and Earth Occultation
means that the dark side
of Jupiter is facing the
sun and earth at
this point.*

Voyager VOYAGER 2 TRAJECTORY

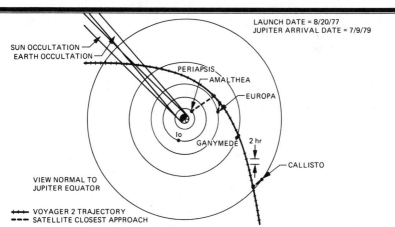

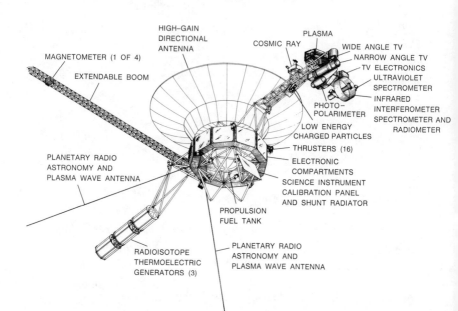

This diagram shows the placement of the spacecraft's instruments.

Science Director Ed Stone often had to use his skills as an arbitrator.
TERRY ANDRUES

Deputy Science Director and chief of the Science Investigation Support Team, Charles Stembridge saw the Voyager project being born, watched it grow and is following its journey through space.
TERRY ANDRUES

Brad Smith, Imaging Team leader. "We're extending our eyes into the unknown."
TERRY ANDRUES

Fred Scarf, whose belief in himself and in his investigation finally paid off.
TERRY ANDRUES

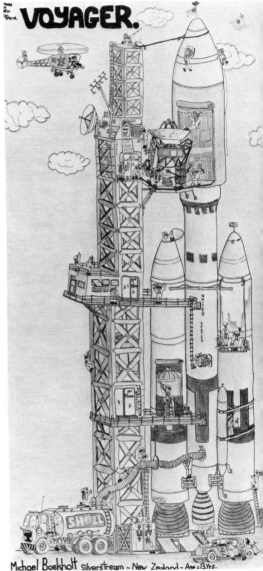

This cartoon of the Voyager launch preparations was drawn by thirteen-year-old Michael Boekholt of Silverstream, New Zealand.

The Goldstone Tracking Station in California is the prime station of NASA's worldwide network, designed and built to monitor unmanned interplanetary spacecraft. The dish of this antenna is 210 feet in diameter.

Dave Durham of the Spacecraft Team found that mistakes occur even in the most carefully planned space mission.
TERRY ANDRUES

[6]

"Mutiny in Space"

R IGHT NOW things don't look good . . . the spacecraft is in trouble."

John Casani would have liked to give some better news to the reporters at the Cape Canaveral press conference. As the Project Manager, he was deeply concerned about the fate of Voyager 2. It had been in flight less than one hour and already seemed bent on destroying itself.

At that point, no one knew exactly what had gone wrong. Why did the spacecraft vibrate so violently as it left the ground? Why did it spin so rapidly when it separated from the Centaur upper stage booster?

During all of this wild activity, the attitude control computer kept commanding the thrusters to fire. Switches were being turned on and off repeatedly, causing the primary and the redundant attitude control systems to alternate. Systems that were supposed to have been activated were not. Others that should have been at rest were in operation. There was a series of "gyro swaps," in which the three gyros took turns trying to keep the spacecraft stable with reference to the Sun, the Earth, and the bright star Canopus. Nothing seemed to be going according to plan.

As the spacecraft emerged from the Earth's atmosphere, its flow of data stopped. This interruption in communication had been expected, because at that point the spacecraft went into a planned maneuver during which its high gain antenna was pointing away from Earth. During such a science or engineering maneuver, the data is picked up by the tape recorder for later transmission. The real time monitors know to the second exactly when they should be able to pick up the spacecraft's signal again.

Glenn Cunningham was in charge of the spacecraft team at Cape Canaveral. He and everyone else in the control room were anxiously awaiting the reappearance of the Voyager data stream. Until then, they wouldn't know whether the spacecraft had survived its rocky launching or not.

DAVE DURHAM of the JPL Spacecraft Team was in Pasadena at launch time. He had grown up with the space age and would never forget Neil Armstrong taking his historic first steps on the Moon.

Now that Dave himself was part of a space mission,

he was greatly puzzled when he saw the things that were going wrong. Before he started working at JPL, he had heard only about the successes of the various missions. He hadn't realized that in the exact world of physics and mathematics there are also many failures. Was Voyager 2 going to be one of them?

MEANWHILE, back at Cape Canaveral Fred Scarf was also deeply concerned about the way the flight was going. He, along with Don Gurnett and Jim Warwick, had been in the control room at the time of the launch. The spacecraft had been ordered to extend the instrument antenna that they were sharing, but there had been no indication that the order had been obeyed. For Fred, the waiting for the signal was almost unbearable. There was a sick feeling deep in his stomach. Had his instrument survived the launching? How long would it be before he knew whether or not it was all right?

Finally, Fred and Don went out to lunch, but they didn't feel any better when they returned to the control room. "I know it's not going to be any good," Don remarked. As he entered the room and shut the door, the spacecraft's signal started coming in loud and clear and his gloom evaporated. The steady click-clack of the teletype printer was the most beautiful sound in the world. A short while later, Don and Fred knew that the antenna was extended and ready to do its job.

At the same time it was obvious that the rough

launch had caused a number of major changes in the condition of the spacecraft. Some of these changes were so damaging to the health of the spacecraft that it sent down an engineering status report of "mort."

Mort means death. Such a report could mean that the spacecraft had been lost.

While the sequencing team began sending up frantic messages ordering the spacecraft to return to its normal operating conditions, other teams of people went to work to find out why the "anomalies," or unexpected events, had happened. They went over all of the sequencing that had been given to the spacecraft. They examined all of the data that had been sent back. Hour after hour, inch by inch, they searched for the answers they knew were contained somewhere in the pages of computer printout. It was urgent that they find out, not only what had happened, but whether or not it would happen again.

Voyager 2 finally responded to the emergency commands from Earth, and at Pasadena Ron Draper of the Mission Planning Office met with a group of reporters. "Things are looking good," he announced.

"You'd better talk to your boss, John Casani, at Cape Canaveral," a reporter said. "Your stories don't agree."

"Well, we've received some updated information," Ron replied. He knew that newspapers thrive on disagreement and controversy.

Actually, the spacecraft was out of danger, but problems were still occurring. About an hour after lift-off the mission controllers should have received a signal to indicate that the seven and a half foot boom that contained the scan platform and several science instruments had "deployed," or extended itself and become securely locked into position. That message didn't arrive. Was the boom still in its launch position, tucked down against the side of the spacecraft? Or was it stuck at some midway point? How could the instruments be pointed and accurately aimed without knowing the exact position of the scan platform? Would their many valuable measurements at the planets and satellites be lost?

"Tiger teams" were hastily assembled at both JPL and Cape Canaveral. The people on those teams worked throughout the night and all through the next day. Two days after launch they sent some commands to the spacecraft. Its cameras were ordered to take several pictures of certain easily identifiable groups of bright stars. When those pictures arrived at JPL, some navigation experts studied them. They found that the scan platform was actually only a fraction of an inch away from fully locked into position.

Later, a rolling maneuver of the spacecraft snapped the boom into place. More pictures taken of the same stars now showed that the aiming of the instruments was exactly as it should be.

Other problems plagued the spacecraft. During the planned "jettison," or throwing off, of the IRIS dust cover, the spacecraft began to turn at a very fast rate. This unexpected movement made the onboard computers think that there was something wrong with the attitude control system. They issued special commands to protect the spacecraft from possible damage. All previously planned activities were halted as the computers waited for man to rescue the spacecraft from the imagined danger.

Without waiting for a full explanation of the incident, some reporters from the *Los Angeles Times* pounced on the story. The newspaper's next edition carried the large, bold front page headline, "MUTINY IN SPACE!"

The truth was that the spacecraft had done exactly what it had been programmed to do under the circumstances. When it senses danger, or isn't sure about what is happening, its computers go into a failure protection mode, suspending operations until the matter has been cleared up.

ALL OF THESE anomalies were putting a lot of pressure on Dave Durham and the other members of Mission Control. Many of them went without sleep for thirty-six hours at a stretch. Those who did go home just grabbed a quick nap and a bite to eat before they rushed back to work. Everyone on the team was totally involved in the task of tracing down the causes of Voyager 2's problems. There was a double-edged reason for their concern. First, these anomalies couldn't be allowed to happen during the Jupiter encounter. Second, if possible, these problems shouldn't be allowed to occur on Voyager 1.

Painstakingly, the sequencers, engineers, and scientists continued to look back over every step of the sequencing and to pore over the endless pages of printout from the spacecraft's computers. Their scientific detective work finally paid off. It became evident that most of the launch problems had been caused by very small errors in the sequencing process. Some of them had occurred because the actual flight conditions differed from the results of the spacecraft's ground testing. For instance, both Voyagers had been programmed to expect much less violent launch vibrations. Confusion had reigned as Voyager 2 fought to maintain its stability despite those vibrations.

A big problem had been solved, and now the team members could return to working their regular hours. Dave Durham was feeling good. These things shouldn't have happened, he thought, but we were able to handle them. The spacecraft's all right, and we know a lot more about it now than we did before.

Dave's feelings reflected those of the group in general. The original panic had changed to a deep satisfaction. They felt a little more confident about their ability to handle any future problems that might come up.

It wasn't long before that confidence was tested. Within a month of the launch, an intermittent series of unexplained thruster firings began to occur. What was causing these "bumps in the night," as they came to be known? The team's working days again grew long as they worked at solving the new problem. Dave began to wonder if there was something basically wrong with the spacecraft's design. Would the flight turn into an unending succession of anomalies?

Again, the problem was solved after hours of looking at every detail of the sequencing. It was found that the Canopus star tracker had a tendency to turn away from Canopus and start tracking particles of matter that just happened to be strongly reflecting the light of the sun. This change triggered the mysterious series of firings.

There had been times when the spacecraft's signal hadn't reappeared as scheduled after a planned maneuver. The first time such an anomaly had occurred, everyone thought that the spacecraft was lost. Concern quickly turned into panic and then despair as the hours of silence continued. Far from giving up, however, the team members spent that time searching for a way to reestablish communication.

They found that some of these lapses had occurred because the spacecraft had been involved in doing some internal checks or in some other activity. Thus, it was unable to return to its correct position relative to earth, and its downlinked signal was delayed.

Most of the time, these lapses were caused by problems at the DSN tracking stations. Perhaps a member of a DSN crew pulled the wrong switch, thus blocking the signal. Maybe the people on duty had misunderstood the frequency or pointing "predicts" for which they were supposed to be looking. In that case, the spacecraft's signal could have been overlooked.

Many times, a telephone call from JPL to the DSN station quickly cleared up the problem. At other times, the "lost" spacecraft wasn't found until it entered the tracking area of the next DSN station, and the crew there was able to pick up its signal.

"Hey, we did it again," said the members of Mission Control whenever they cleared up an anomaly. The feeling that they could cope with whatever went wrong continued to grow. They now knew the spacecraft itself was basically sound. Taking care of problems was just a matter of staying calm and tracking down their causes little by little.

It wasn't long before the word "panic" disappeared from the team's vocabulary.

NOW THAT Voyager 2 seemed to be all right, it was time to start thinking about Voyager 1. It was scheduled for launch in just four more days. Would its scan platform boom also cause problems during its deployment? Would there be the same trouble with the IRIS dust cover? Would the spacecraft lose its stability right after lift-off?

No one wanted to go through all of those things

again. It was agreed that preventive and corrective measures should be taken. But how could the work be done by September 1? Was it safe to postpone the launch date? The answer to that question became the responsibility of Charley Kohlhase.

Actually, Charley reasoned, a small delay might be a good thing. All of the trajectories on the various days required a major correction maneuver as the spacecraft left Jupiter for Saturn. But the September 1 launch date would require a bigger maneuver than the later launch days. In fact, for every day the launch was delayed, that maneuver would require ten pounds less fuel; thus, there would be a reserve in case of an emergency.

On the other hand, Charley realized that waiting meant taking a chance that the weather wouldn't hold out. What if a storm moved in over the Cape at the last minute? What if something failed during a final countdown check? Before the weather cleared, or before the repairs could be made, the launch period would be over. Voyager 1 would never get off the ground.

Charley thought some more, then made some calculations. He discussed the matter with engineers and scientists. Finally he told John Casani that he thought it would be a good idea to postpone the launch. The fuel savings, plus the chance to correct the spacecraft's problems, outweighed the possible disadvantages of the later launch date. September 5 was chosen for lift-off.

* * *

UNLIKE its sister ship, Voyager 1 had a seemingly uneventful first few minutes of flight. It had been reprogrammed to expect the high-rate Titan roll maneuver as it left the launch pad. Right on schedule the first-stage Titan rockets burned out, then were jettisoned into the Atlantic Ocean. The main liquid propellant engine of the Titan continued to thrust the spacecraft through its second stage of powered flight.

The third stage Centaur fired up for several minutes, then shut itself down. Now it was carrying Voyager 1 through a forty-five minute "parking orbit" one hundred and four miles above Earth.

Just before that shutdown, the flight engineers noticed that there was something wrong. The Titan main engine had shut down early, and the Centaur wasn't following its exact second-to-second programmed instructions. As a result of the Titan problem, the Centaur had to burn longer to make up for the speed the Titan had failed to provide.

As even more worrisome fact was that the Centaur was using its fuel up faster than had been expected.

Fifteen minutes into the parking orbit, the mission controllers realized that the Centaur had burned 1,200 pounds more fuel than it should have. At the time, no one knew the reason for this huge consumption, but at that point it didn't make any difference. There was nothing anyone could do about it. While some people crossed their fingers, the engineers made some quick calculations. When they were through, they announced that they thought the fuel would hold out through the "insertion" burn.

Even under the best of conditions, the moment of trajectory insertion is a delicate operation. The rocket's guidance system has to figure out the exact spot at which the insertion should occur. It must then figure out just how much "kick" to give the spacecraft. Voyager 1 had to begin its flight to Jupiter at 34,000 miles an hour. If it went much slower, it wouldn't reach its target. If it went much faster, it would overshoot the planet.

The Centaur's fuel did hold out, but just barely. There was less than five seconds' worth in its tank after it had boosted Voyager 1 on its way to Jupiter and detached itself.

Now the spacecraft was on its own. A few minutes later, like a mighty schooner setting sail, it began to deploy the rest of its booms and antennas. The down-linked data stream came in clearly and without interruption. Voyager 1 was on its way!

JUST HOW MUCH of the success of this launch lay in the latest scientific and engineering skill, and how much of it lay in good old-fashioned luck? The spacecraft engineers had shown foresight in having some reserve fuel tanks on board the Centaur. But what if the rocket had emptied its tanks just six seconds sooner? No amount of engineering skill could have put the spacecraft into its insertion corridor.

And wasn't it luck, after all, that had caused the delay in the launch of Voyager 1? After it was launched, the engineers realized that each time the thrusters burned, they were using up twenty percent more fuel than they should have. Without that extra forty pounds saved by the change in launch date, the spacecraft might never have made it to Saturn.

The people who work on a space project can't explain why some things happen as they do. They do the best job they can. Sometimes all they can do is to keep their fingers crossed and hope their luck holds out. In the case of the Voyager project, it did.

[7]

The Loop—People, Computers, People

THE MEN & WOMEN who work on a space project know that in the end it will be their skills and knowledge, not luck, that make the difference between success and failure. Even so, some of their accomplishments seem to be touched with wizardry.

As an example, what if you were strong enough to throw a basketball from where you're standing to a point hundreds of miles away? Stretch your imagination a little more and picture yourself sinking the shot. Not only that, but the ball doesn't even touch the rim of the hoop. Remarkable accuracy? Of course. No one would blame you for feeling proud of yourself.

Members of the Voyager Mission Operations team perform this sort of magic every day. The two spacecraft may be a half billion miles away, and hurtling through space at fifteen to twenty miles per second, yet these people control them with the same degree of accuracy that your fantastic basketball shot would have to have had.

The mission operations process has four parts to it. One of them is mission control, or "real time monitoring," in which the science and engineering data are watched as they come into the Space Flight Operations Center at JPL. The men and women doing this monitoring have to be alert for signs of trouble. If something goes wrong, the sooner a message is sent up to tell the spacecraft what to do, the better.

Another part is the "non-real time" analysis, in which experts study big blocks of data several hours or several days after they've been received. In this way, they can detect slowly developing trends that weren't noticeable during the real time monitoring. Some of these trends can spell trouble. Others may reveal an exciting scientific discovery.

A third part of mission operations—the navigation of the spacecraft—is thought by many people to be the most exciting job on the project. Every day during the main encounter periods the two Voyagers send down several navigation pictures, which show their positions relative to certain stars. The members of the navigation team study these pictures. If they see that one of the spacecraft is slowly drifting off course, the flight engineers will order it to fire its thrusters. A slight "burn" of the thrusters on the right side will gently guide the spacecraft to the left. The left hand thrusters will nudge it to the right. Similarly, speed can be changed by thrusting forward to slow or aft to speed up. The guiding of the Voyagers during their Jupiter encounters was a tricky business. No champion slalom skier ever had to maneuver more accurately.

A COMPUTER'S storage area can hold only a certain number of instructions at one time. As each Voyager uses up one block, or set, of commands, another has to be uplinked to replace it. Dave Linick was the leader of the Voyager Sequencing team, which is responsible for keeping the computer supplied with instructions. Sequencing is the fourth part of mission operations. Dave thinks it's the most interesting part. The idea of commanding a spacecraft that's hundreds of millions of miles away fascinates him.

The sequencers collect the new instructions from the scientists and their support people, and from the flight engineers. They then translate them into computer language and transmit them. As each Voyager neared Jupiter, its onboard computer began to issue more and more instructions each day. Soon a command load was lasting only one day. During the near approach and encounter periods, the sequencing team worked around the clock. Sending up the commands was like pouring water into a barrel with a partially open spigot. It was a race against time.

During a cruise phase between planets or encounters, the sequencers can work in a more leisurely manner. If an emergency occurs, however, it means more sleepless nights.

All of the uplinked messages enter the spacecraft through its "front door," the radio receiver. The receiver is always turned on, but most of the time it's listening only to "cosmic static." This static is radio noise that's caused by the violent actions of normal stars, exploding stars, and colliding galaxies. Such sounds fill the reaches of outer space, and both Voyagers are programmed to ignore them.

A command message has a different "feel" to it, because it's formed into a definite pattern and has a "leading identifier." This carefully arranged stream of data letters, or "bits," is like a knock on the door of the spacecraft. It's a signal that man is trying to get its attention.

The commands go through the receiver into the spacecraft's "postal service" and command center, a special computer called the CCS (Command Control Subsystem). The CCS computer is the brains of the spacecraft. It stores the received commands in its memory until the time on the clock timer inside the CCS matches the time tag on the stored command. The computer delivers the command to the correct "address," or destination on board the spacecraft. The command then causes some specific action to occur.

A real time command has a "special delivery" code on it. The CCS knows that it has to be passed on immediately.

If the command is a real time engineering command, it may go to the AACS (the Attitude and Articulation Control Subsystem). This computer serves as an automated engineer to control the amount of propulsion that keeps the spacecraft stable and on course. The AACS also moves the scan platform from one pointing position to another. Most of the programming for its commands was loaded into its memory before launch. Those instructions are called into action throughout the flight either by the CCS or by direct commands from Earth.

Many real time science commands are sent to the Flight Data Subsystem (FDS). This computer controls some parts of the scientific instruments. It's the official collector and dispatcher of all of the scientific and engineering data. During the cruise phase, it uses the S-band frequency to send back the results of the low-rate scientific observations. It also sends back a slow, continuous stream of engineering information. This steady, forty-bit-per-second "heartbeat" tells the mission operations people about the spacecraft's health. At any one time. they know its temperature, whether or not it's stable, and how much fuel it has left.

During the Jupiter encounter phase, the FDS

worked feverishly at the X-band rate to send back its torrent of scientific information. The people at the DSN stations had to be ready to receive this flood of data. At each station there are at least two antennas. The larger ones have "dishes," or "ears," that are sixty-four meters (210 feet) across. They are used during encounter because they can receive both S- and X-band signals with great sensitivity. The smaller ones are twenty-six meters (eighty-five feet) across. They receive only the S-band signal and are used primarily during the cruise phases.

The data leave the DSN receiving station by means of a cable that leads directly into a NASA switching area, and then into the JPL Space Flight Operations Center. There a computer decodes the data, recognizes the different types of information, and speeds each one to the right department. The engineers get the spacecraft's health reports, the imaging team gets its pictures, and the other science investigators get their measurements.

New command loads are sent to the spacecraft from the Space Flight Operations Center. Thus it's here that the invisible loop of communication between man and machine begins and ends.

THE GREATER the distance between the spacecraft and Earth, the more difficult and remarkable the job of the Mission Operations team becomes. Jupiter is 500 million miles away from Earth, and it takes about forty-five minutes to uplink a command over that distance. At Saturn that time is doubled.

Because of this great time lag, both spacecraft were designed to take care of themselves as much as possible. Since they are such independent, highly intelligent machines, it's easy to forget that without people they would be worthless. If one of the Voyagers gets into trouble, all it can do is go into a failure protection mode, suspend its activities, protect the science instruments and wait for man to come to the rescue.

It's true that a person can make a mistake and tell the spacecraft to do something stupid or harmful. Someone could instruct an instrument to point in the wrong direction during an encounter time. As a result of that human error, the instrument couldn't gather any data. Or another delicate instrument could be told to point itself directly at the sun, an act which might destroy it. Voyagers 1 and 2 know that these instructions are illegal. They would immediately reject them.

Pretty smart? Not really. It was human beings who told them that these things were wrong in the first place. And it's people, after all, who run the show, and who go without sleep to solve the problems that can plague any space mission.

[8]

A Small Group with a Big Voice

AS THE VOYAGER flights progressed, the project people had proved themselves capable of coping with the unusual problems that occurred on board the spacecraft. Meanwhile another more commonplace problem had begun to plague Ray Heacock, who was now the Project Manager. Ray had taken the reins from John Casani when John left to work on another project.

Somehow, over the course of the coming year, Ray was going to have to cut 1 million dollars off the cost of operating the spacecraft and of processing their data. If he didn't, there might not be enough money to do a good Saturn encounter. There was a possibility that Congress would eventually give the project more funding, but right now everyone was going to have to start cutting corners. The economizing had to be done in a way that wouldn't make too much of a dent in the mission's science return. To get some help in solving this problem, Ray called a meeting of the Science Steering Group (SSG).

The SSG is a small group of people that has a big voice in the project planning. It consists of the eleven Principal Investigators (PI's) and the Project Scientist, Ed Stone, who is the chairman of the Voyager Steering Group.

Ray opened the meeting with a few remarks. "We just don't have the money to do everything that we wanted to do during the Jupiter encounter," he said. "What are your ideas about ways to cut back?"

"Maybe we can do fewer interplanetary samplings during the Earth-Jupiter Cruise phase," suggested Norm Ness, the magnetometer team's PI. "My instrument seems quite stable, and a few less full turn maneuvers shouldn't cause any serious problems."

"Well," said Herb Bridge, another PI, "we can probably get by with six samplings instead of ten, but I'm not happy about it. That's the only way my instrument can sample the areas that our sensors don't usually see. Cutting back may cause real difficulty in comparing the conditions between Jupiter and Saturn with those between Earth and Jupiter."

Herb was silent for a moment, then he shrugged. "But I guess I can make do. Have you checked out the other areas of the project for possible savings, Ray?"

Ray nodded. "Yes. We've simplified some procedures and cut back in several support areas. Reducing the number of maneuvers would save us the cost of a tracking antenna twice a month, and we wouldn't have to call up as many of the crew. We'd save about $200,000 with that cutback."

Ed Stone spoke up. "What would happen if we held off taking measurements of the Jupiter atmosphere awhile longer? We could start when we're only sixty days away instead of ninety."

Ray scribbled some figures on a piece of paper. "We'd save at least $40,000 there by not having to do a computer load to sequence that thirty-day period."

"But how much would we be losing in the way of good science data?" asked Brad Smith, head of the Imaging team. "Remember, no ground-based instruments can see what Voyager will be able to see when it's ninety days out from Jupiter. Instead of cutting the front end, why don't we cut down our *post*-Jupiter sets of measurements?"

Another PI made a suggestion. "How many man hours can we eliminate? Couldn't we cut out the night shift at this point? We all feel a little more confident about our instruments now. Maybe we don't have to keep such a close watch over them."

There were more questions, more replies, more objections, more doubts. The end result was that the one million dollars was saved, and very little science was sacrificed. Every one was relieved, because science, after all, is what a planetary space mission is all about.

THIS SCENE is partially fictitious, but similar ones occur many times during any space flight. As the science experts, the members of the SSG have to be consulted about anything that might affect the spacecraft's scientific investigations. Not all of the problems are easily resolved. Many times there are heated discussions among the PI's as to who should give up viewing time and when. The most cool-headed scientist can become emotional when the decision threatens a measurement that is important to him.

Ed Stone is a skilled arbiter. Even so, there are times when he's forced to make the final decision himself because two or more PI's can't come to an agreement. His judgment had much to do with the choosing of the Voyager trajectories. Every member of the SSG favored at least one flight path over the others because it gave his instrument a better viewing angle of Io, or more time to observe the details of Jupiter's atmosphere. One trajectory might have been excellent because it passed close to Ganymede, or Io's flux tube, a region that contains enormous electrical currents flowing in space between Jupiter and Io. Another was better for imaging, because it had a close encounter with four satellites instead of only two.

Like a jury, the SSG had to deliberate on each of these points. It had to choose a pair of trajectories that gave the most science yield for all of the investigations, and yet still satisfied the engineers' navigation requirements.

Next, the group had to decide what scientific observations to perform in each "time slot," or period.

Putting all of the PI's requests into the limited time around encounter is a tricky job. It took a year to plan the details of the one forty hour period nearest Jupiter. Every minute had to be studied, torn apart, discussed, argued over, and often traded off between one PI and another.

"Look," the infrared investigator, Rudy Hanel, might have said. "I have only seven minutes to make that observation. I have to have twenty. There's no way I can get a good signal to noise ratio in less time."

Lyle Broadfoot, who has the ultraviolet instrument on Voyager, interrupted. "But you don't have to worry about your signal to noise ratio in that part of the spectrum if you're only going to measure hydrogen and helium. On the other hand, just look at the problem *I* have during that period."

Lonne Lane as Assistant Project Scientist had the major responsibility for the encounter sequence design. "Let's see what we can do to get this straightened out," he said. "Maybe we can move this observation up to this time slot."

Someone else objected. "That interferes with *my* investigation, Lonne. You're not giving the scan platform enough time to change position."

"Don't panic. I've thought about that. Look here's how it will work . . ."

The trade-offs go on and on. The photopolarimeter has to get up closer to get good data from small regions. At the same time, the cameras have to be far enough back to get pictures of a wide area of the atmosphere. Little by little, the problems were untangled and the encounter time was parceled out.

Then a few days later Reta Beebe, an astronomer, called from New Mexico. Her observations had shown that the Great Red Spot had shifted its position. Both the SSG and the Science Integration Team had to go back to the drawing board to adjust the time period that was affected by this discovery. There were more trade-offs, more discussions, more compromises. Within a week, some other discovery might be made that would start the whole process over again.

NOT ALL of the SSG meetings are held because of this kind of problem. Many times the members gather to exchange ideas, to ask for help, and to give each other support. All of the PI's are good scientists, but they have different backgrounds and experiences. What one of them lacks, another can often supply. Maybe an investigator is puzzled about how to interpret his latest data return.

By asking the SSG, he can get ideas from several other experts. Usually, at least one of these ideas will shed light on his dilemma. At the next meeting he himself might have just the information that someone else needs.

By this pooling of knowledge, each PI finds that he can come to a better understanding of his own specialty. The members of the Voyager Science Steering Group know that there are very few contemporary scientists working alone in isolated laboratories. In this fast-moving world most of them want and need the help and support of their fellow scientists. In return, they themselves want to share the things that they have learned. Without this sort of collaboration, we could not have entered the space age.

[9]

"A Kettle of Bubbling Bright Paint"

WHILE THE VOYAGER project people were overcoming their budget problems, the two spacecraft were forging ahead into the far reaches of space. By December 15, they were 78 million miles away from Earth. At that time, because of its shorter trajectory and its slightly higher rate of speed, Voyager 1 was pulling ahead of its sister ship.

Both spacecraft spent nine months crossing the supposedly hazardous asteroid belt, a vast ring of space litter that encircles the sun beyond the orbit of Mars. They passed through the belt without being damaged, just as the two Pioneers had. Scientists now knew that the asteroid belt is not an impenetrable wall. Instead, in most places, it is more like a thin curtain.

Periodically, the Voyagers tested their instruments and exercised their scan platforms. At selected times they gathered and transmitted information about the distant magnetic fields of the sun and the charged particles that are emitted from the sun.

IN THE FALL of 1978 a human error set in motion a series of events that could have ended the usefulness of Voyager 2. It all started when someone forgot to send up a command that the spacecraft had been programmed to expect. When the command didn't arrive, the CCS assumed that the primary receiver wasn't working. In response, it switched to the backup, or "redundant" receiver.

When the mission controllers realized what had happened, they ordered the spacecraft to return to its primary receiver. At that point, they found that there was something wrong with the redundant receiver. It was accepting commands on only a very limited frequency range, and that range seemed to vary from time to time. The sequencers had a difficult time figuring out what frequency to use.

Having a defective redundant receiver was a serious enough problem. When it finally accepted a command, the mission controllers found they had an even more serious problem. The primary receiver wasn't working at all. It had "died."

By this time, the people on the Voyager project were

used to having things go wrong. They were becoming hardened veterans in the continuing war on anomalies. Since they had faced problems before and had overcome them, they knew there must be a way to overcome this one. All it took was a lot of work and more sleepless nights.

Two days later some experts on the radio system found a way to predict the frequency upon which messages would be accepted by the receiver. They tested their method by sending up several commands until they were certain that their messages would get through.

But the spacecraft still had only one receiver. Going into a planet encounter with this handicap would be extremely risky. In case that receiver also died, the sequencers prepared some special command blocks and sent them to the spacecraft. The CCS was told to use those instructions only if it stopped hearing from Earth. The encounter situation wouldn't be as good if the mission controllers couldn't communicate directly with Voyager 2. Nevertheless, those backup sequences would enable the spacecraft to complete its Jupiter mission with some degree of success.

THE MISSION CONTROLLERS were kept busy caring for the day-to-day needs of the spacecraft and coping with its emergencies. Meanwhile, hundreds of other people were gearing up for the Jupiter encounter. They had to get an early start, because there was a tremendous amount of work to do. The closer the spacecraft got to the planet, the more information there was upon which to base the instructions. The sequencers kept busy changing, updating, and adjusting the thousands of commands that would be needed.

Finally, three months before closest approach, the scientists and engineers had their last chance to make any major changes in the sequencing. The remaining time had to be used for testing. By feeding the command blocks into a JPL computer, the sequencers could perform a "dress rehearsal" of the encounter. At that time, any illegal or confusing orders would be kicked out by the computer and could then be corrected.

MEANWHILE, at the Ames Research Center in Northern California, another group of people were preparing for a busy time. They were the members of the Pioneer-Venus teams. That spacecraft would soon be entering an orbit around Venus, and it too would be downlinking a stream of valuable information.

When the leaders of this project and the Voyager project leaders realized that both of their spacecraft would be in the same tracking station area at the same time, they knew they had a problem. The DSN antenna could point in only one direction at one time. Which spacecraft should it track? It was now time for some mission-to-mission trade-offs. Scientists, engineers, and sequencers from both projects started a series of meetings to find a reasonable solution. Time was short, and there was a lot of work to do.

AT THE BEGINNING of its Jupiter far encounter, Voyager 1 was eighty days away from the great planet. The sequencers uplinked a block of commands which said, in effect, "Vacation's over. Time to get to work!" Soon the imaging system would be taking the first of thousands of pictures of the planet and its satellites. The other instruments would start to probe the atmosphere, pointing first in one direction, then another, like a pack of bloodhounds on the scent.

The "vacation" was over for the people involved in the project too. Mission controllers, science teams, engineers, DSN crews—everyone was being scheduled and prepared to receive the torrent of data that would soon be pouring toward Earth. Forty-hour weeks turned into eighty-hour marathons.

In December of 1978 the first intriguing pictures of Jupiter began to filter through the JPL computer. Closed-circuit television sets were placed in the cafeteria and in many offices. Scientists and secretaries, engineers and technicians, librarians and security guards clustered in front of them to see the images that had been sent from a distance of 400 million miles.

Brad Smith expressed the way many of them felt. "We're extending our eyes into the unknown. Not since Mariner 4, some fifteen years ago, have we been less prepared, less certain of what we expect to see."

Others weren't able to say it quite so well. "Can you imagine?" "Would you look at that . . . and that?" and "Wow!" were the murmured comments that were passed back and forth. All of them told of the feeling of magic in the air.

The members of the SSG were interpreting the scientific data that were coming from the spacecraft, then holding press conferences to answer reporters' questions and to release the latest information. Each day they picked the most interesting and colorful pictures out of the hundreds that had been received. The next day those photos were being viewed by people all over the world.

As encounter time drew near, daily meetings were held in JPL's von Karman Auditorium, and television programs featured Ed Stone, Garry Hunt, Hal Masursky, and other scientists. These men became the links between the mission and the people of the world.

THE CLOSER the spacecraft got to Jupiter, the more obvious it became that the huge planet had changed a lot since the Pioneers' visit five years earlier. One thing was clear—Jupiter's atmosphere wasn't the stable, well organized environment that the Pioneer 10 pictures had made it out to be. There was constant movement as clouds swirled toward each other, touched, then drifted apart. Within these clouds, puffs and whirlpools played, and a variety of specks and spots appeared and disappeared. The bands that encircled the planet turned out to be swiftly flowing gaseous jet streams. Eddies and whorls conflicted with the main current, causing an even higher level of turmoil.

The movement was exciting to watch, but the brilliant coloring was even more so. Oranges competed with golds and reds and blues. There were pinks and shadings of bronze and amber. The entire planet appeared as a cosmic rainbow of pulsating hues. One writer described it as "a kettle of bubbling bright paints that would not mix."

MARCH 5 was to be the day of the Voyager 1's closest encounter. As it drew near, all of the Principal Investigators and some of their team members were at JPL busily monitoring their instruments. The Lab's halls were filled with reporters and science writers, and the cafeteria extended its hours to feed the hungry crowds. As the neighboring hillside communities slept, the lights of JPL blazed, its computers spewed forth data, and its telephone lines crackled with urgent dialogs.

Voyager 1 was now hurtling toward its target at the rate of 600,000 miles a day. The closer it got, the more excitement, enthusiasm, and optimism was expressed at the daily press briefings. Underlying these emotions, there were often unspoken doubts and fears. How many dangerous surprises are lying in wait for the tiny spacecraft? Will it be "fried" when it enters Jupiter's trapped radiation field? What will that intense radiation do to its sensitive instruments and computer parts? Will the spacecraft be able to follow all of the complicated instructions that it holds in its computer memory?

And what about the conflicts with the Venus mission? From now on we can give the Venus spacecraft only an hour or two of tracking time each day. But if Pioneer Venus declares an emergency, what then?

FEBRUARY 26 came and went, and the scientists had something else to puzzle over. According to their calculations, Voyager 1 should have passed through the Jupiter "bowshock" on that date. The bowshock is an invisible boundary in space. It's here that the charged particles of the solar wind meet Jupiter's magnetic field, which is like a huge bubble encasing the planet and its moons. Just before this meeting, the solar wind is traveling a million miles an hour. When it hits the edge of the magnetic field, it's suddenly forced to slow down to 400,-000 miles an hour. At that time, the particles are deflected and flow up, down, and around the magnetic field. This "collision" produces a shock wave, much like the one produced by a bullet as it speeds through the air. As the name "bowshock" implies, it's an area of great turbulence. Everyone on the Voyager project was eager to see how the spacecraft would respond to this part of its journey.

Finally, after two more days of anxious waiting, a

message arrived from Australia. At seven o'clock that morning, the Voyager 1 had punched through the bow-shock and appeared to be undamaged by the experience. During the next few hours, the changing velocity of the solar wind pushed the edge of the magnetosphere to and fro. As a result, the spacecraft had to endure five more crossings of the bowshock. It still appeared to be un-damaged.

The air of expectancy that had pervaded the Lab for months, and which had been steadily increasing over the past several weeks, was now replaced with a sense of urgency. Voyager 1 was no longer just *getting* there. It was *there!* Close encounter had begun.

On Friday, March 2, there were cheers in the mission control room when the spacecraft unhesitatingly obeyed a command to do a complete roll. During the maneuver, its instruments got a chance to study all the "faces" of the surrounding magnetic environment and its trapped radiation. Despite the fact that it was being bombarded by this radiation, the Voyager performed like a seasoned soldier under fire.

The scientific world was fascinated by the bowshock and by Jupiter's magnetic field, but it was the imaging team's pictures that continued to awe the rest of the world. Suddenly the Great Red Spot, that eternal storm, that pulsing, gassy blob, was as close as the nearest tele-vision screen. For the first time Amalthea was seen to be a "little potato" of a moon, instead of an abandoned spaceship as some people had imagined it to be. People everywhere were peering through Jupiter's "windows" to get a glimpse of its mysterious lower cloud layers.

During its action-packed Jupiter encounter, Voyager 1 took a few seconds to make a gamble. Some scientists had prepared a sequence that was based on a few puzzling measurements that Pioneer had made at Jupiter, plus some shrewd scientific guesses. The sequence instructed the cameras to take a couple of extra pictures in a certain area near the planet. Some people felt that those pictures might reveal the existence of a Jovian ring of debris, much like the ones that encircle Saturn and Uranus. Other scientists doubted that anything like that would show up, but as long as the spacecraft was up there anyway, it might as well take a look.

ON THE EVE of March 4, California's governor, Jerry Brown, joined other notable people who had come to JPL to be present for the Voyager's closest Jupiter encounter. The spacecraft put on a spectacular performance for them. It swept through a celestial corridor, coming to within 173,000 miles of the giant planet. Whipped along by the mighty gravitational pull, it reached speeds of 84,000 miles an hour. Voyager 1 behaved as if it were being guided by a daredevilish, but very expert stunt pilot. It banked steeply around Jupiter, dove under Io, and soared above Ganymede and Callisto. Like rubbernecking tourists, its instruments turned in every direction to take pictures and measurements. At the rate of 115,-000 bits per second, the data came streaming down to Earth.

Right on schedule, the thrusters fired so Voyager could do its special measurements on Jupiter's dark side. Several hours later they fired again so the spacecraft could regain its proper position relative to Earth.

Like Christmas Day, closest approach was over too soon. Voyager 1, having completed its extraordinary feat, slowed down to a little over 50,000 miles an hour. At the last minute, it looked over its shoulder to take some pictures of a location near Amalthea where other small Jovian moons were thought to exist.

After completing that final task, the spacecraft plunged into the darkness of space. Saturn, its next destination, lay 500 million miles down the road. As Voyager 1 began its long cruise, the people at JPL were just beginning to open the surprise packages with which it had showered Earth.

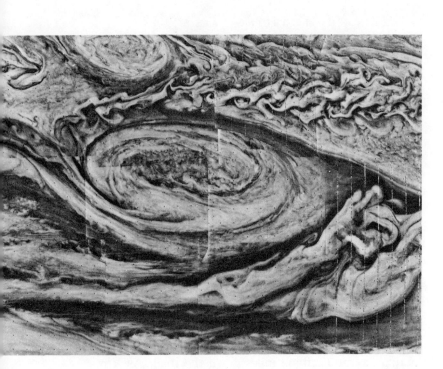

This mosaic of the Great Red Spot was assembled from photos taken by Voyager 1 when it was 1.1 million miles away from Jupiter. The smallest clouds visible in the pictures are 20 miles across.

Ray Amorose of Space Flight Operations helped to guide the two Voyagers through some difficult situations.

Dave Linick, chief of the Sequence Team, believes that man must not give up the opportunity to explore space.
TERRY ANDRUES

Glenn Cunningham, the leader of the Voyager Spacecraft Team, discusses a problem with Conrad Tempe (left), a telecommunications analyst.

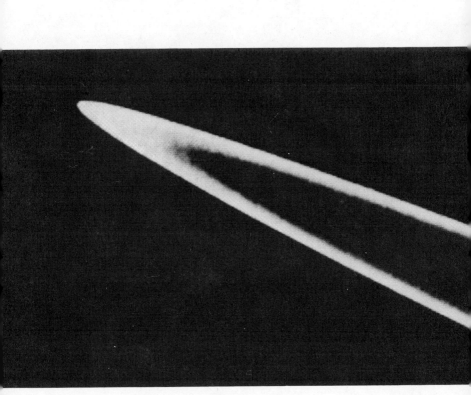

This spectacular view of Jupiter's ring was recorded by Voyager 2. The ring had been discovered by Voyager 1.

This diagram shows the change in the data from the plasma wave instrument that signaled the eagerly awaited crossing of the bowshock.

The imaging team must assemble the final pictures from many smaller ones that the spacecraft sends back. Here are the pictures that were put together to form the complete photograph of Jupiter's ring.

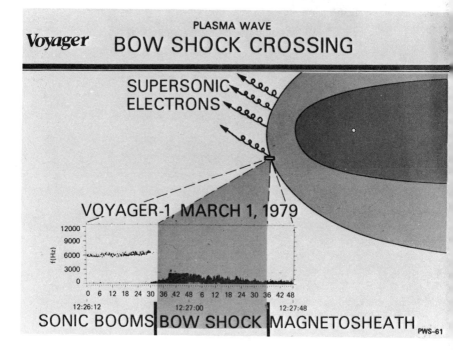

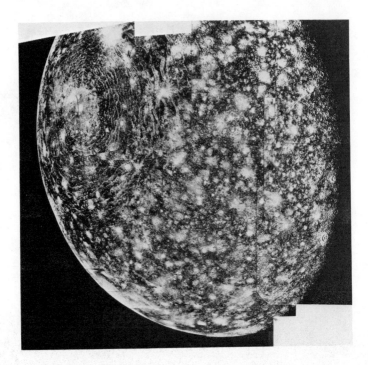

This "photomosaic" of Callisto
was taken by the cameras on
Voyager 1. Callisto probably has
the oldest surface of any of
Jupiter's satellites and has been
heavily cratered by meteorite
impacts.

Europa was Jupiter's smallest known moon before the Voyager flights and it is the brightest. Its icy surface has many cracks, which are filled with a dark material that seems to come from its interior.

This close-up view of Io shows features as small as six miles.

Several pictures were assembled to make up this view of Jupiter's south pole. The dark hole in the center represents a space for which no pictures were taken. The numbers mark Jupiter's latitudes.

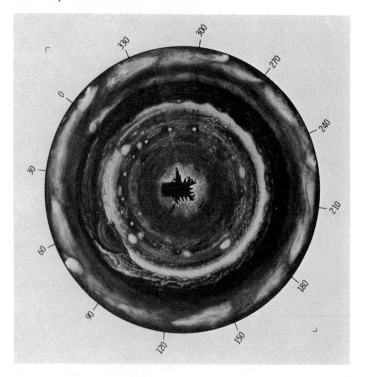

This Voyager 1 image was taken of Jupiter's dark side. The long bright streak is an aurora, similar to our northern lights. The other bright spots are thought to be lightning. These flashes are comparable to the brightness of superbolts at the tops of Earth's tropical thunderstorms.

Linda Morabito, whose questions about a mysterious plume led to the discovery of an outer space volcano.
DAVID SMALLS

This picture was taken by Voyager 2
during the volcano watch. The plume
seen here on the dark (right) rim of Io is
about 115 miles high and 202 miles wide.
The intensity of this eruption was 1½
times greater than it had been when
Voyager 1 flew by.

Two close-up pictures of Ganymede taken on the same day by Voyager 2. They show different views of dark, heavily cratered terrain. The top photo was taken from a distance of 86,000 miles, the bottom, from a distance of 192,000 miles.

Ron Draper of the Spacecraft Team studies a report as he prepares for the Voyager Saturn encounter.

Saturn's F ring was photographed from a distance of 470,000 miles. The braided ring effect has raised many questions. It seems to be obeying laws of orbital mechanics that remain unknown to scientists.

The complex structure of Saturn's rings can be seen in this picture, which was taken from a distance of five million miles. The fourteenth satellite of Saturn, which was discovered by Voyager 1, can be seen just inside the narrow, outermost, F ring at the upper left.

The crescent of Saturn, the planet's rings, and their shadows are seen in this image that was taken on November 13, 1980, from a distance of 930,000 miles. The shadow of the rings causes the dark band across the crescent of the planet.

Saturn and its satellites Tethys (outer left), Enceladus (inner left) and Mimas (lower right) are seen in this Voyager photograph taken from a distance of 11 million miles.

[10]

Creating New Myths

THROUGHOUT every phase of the Jupiter encounter, data tape after data tape had been rushed along a special communication line from JPL to Maryland's Goddard Space Flight Center. Goddard is the home base of the Voyager magnetometer team, and three other Eastern based teams also use the facilities at the Center.

Other data had been sent along communication lines to the University of Colorado and to Tucson, Arizona. There's also a special "hot line" from these two centers to JPL. If someone wants some quick information, he can dial a telephone and be connected directly to a Lab computer. This computer will then relay the latest data from the spacecraft. Fred Scarf's data tapes were sped by courier to the Los Angeles International Airport. From there, they were flown to Iowa City, where they were picked up by a member of the plasma wave team and rushed to the University of Iowa.

All of the members of each team analyzed their data as fast as possible. When they understood it, they sent their results back to JPL. As the encounter progressed, these data findings were used to update the sequences. If an instrument started gathering some unexpected and valuable information, the new sequences would allow it more viewing time.

The analysis of the data was useful in other ways too. For instance, during the two-day search for the bow-shock, each JPL real time monitor kept an eye out for any strange or unidentifiable "wigglings" in the down-linked data. When such markings were seen, all of the PI's were notified. "Look for these lines in your next batch of data," they were told. "Tell us what you think. Is it the bowshock?"

THE IRIS TEAM is one of those that works out of Goddard. Its members have the most difficult time ana-lyzing their data. The IRIS instrument measures, among other things, the energy balance and temperatures of the planets. The information that it collects is received by the JPL computer in a form that can't be interpreted by most scientists. The strange patterns don't make any sense until they have been put through a very long and com-plicated computer program. Only then can the data be understood by scientists and engineers.

Much of the imaging and radio science data is analyzed at JPL. Unlike the data of the IRIS team, computers can take the data bits that form a picture and reconstruct them within a minute or two of their arrival. During the Jupiter encounter, these pictures were being flashed onto television screens almost as soon as they came into the Lab. Nevertheless, since Voyager 1 alone took about 18,000 pictures, months would pass before all of them were studied in great detail.

Specially selected Voyager pictures were printed in newspapers and magazines all over the world. To most people, they will always be the best known part of the entire mission. The Jovian moons have become almost as familiar as our own moon, and just as our moon does, they have inspired some poetic thoughts. One reporter described them as "cosmic Christmas ornaments on a string, dangling in space."

Brad Smith wasn't quite so poetic. When he showed the first close up picture of Io to some reporters, many of them gasped in admiration. Brad looked at the small moon with its surface markings of white mixed with shades of red and orange and said, "I've seen better looking pizzas."

Callisto revealed an icy crust that is dotted with meteorite craters, and Europa looks like a billiard ball with stripes criss-crossing it. Ganymede is marred by tracks that look as if hundreds of dune buggies and dirt bikes had raced across parts of its surface.

The pictures show that each moon has its own

unique character. "There's no such thing as a boring Galilean satellite," said Larry Soderblom, of the imaging team.

One of the most exciting pictures wasn't of a moon or even of the huge planet. It was the one that showed the fuzzy outline of a thin, flat ring around Jupiter. The imaging team's eleven-minute gamble had paid off.

Fred Scarf's persistence and his faith in his plasma wave investigation had paid off too. He had managed to wangle more viewing time for his instrument and he was able to add still more observations when the sequencers used his instrument output to fill in certain parts of the downlinked data stream.

It was during those unexpected extra minutes that Fred got some of his most valuable measurements. His instrument was able to pick up the radio noises that Jim Warwick's planetary radio astronomy experiment wasn't able to detect. Some of these sounds result from the waves set up by physical events that occur in the plasma in space. Other sounds represent the density of electrons in the surrounding space.

One of these cosmic noises sounded like a chorus of chirping birds. Another was a startling sound that Fred called a "whistler." The whistlers result from the waves that are caused by lightning bolts in Jupiter's atmosphere.

"To me, hearing those whistlers was the most exciting part of the whole mission," Fred remarked.

The imaging team later took pictures of the lightning bolts on the dark side of Jupiter. The finding of lightning near Io was a surprise to everyone on the project. Its presence still hasn't been fully explained.

Hour by hour new discoveries were made. Brad Smith suggested that all of the old theories about Jupiter be thrown into a trash can. "We are like students going into an exam thinking we know all the answers, and then going blank," he said. "We just don't know what to make of it."

ALL OF THE INVESTIGATORS presented their findings at the daily science meetings that were held at JPL during the entire encounter period. At these meetings everyone gave a "status report," in which they told about the results of the previous day. They also exchanged information about the data they had analyzed, and asked question about things that they didn't understand. As they discussed the many surprising facts that Voyager 1 was revealing, everyone realized that Brad Smith had been right. Old theories were indeed being thrown into the trash can.

Before any new theories could be developed to replace them, ideas had to be tested and retested. Did this person "read" his data correctly? Aren't there other aspects to consider before he can be sure of what he actually saw? Does that measurement apply to the whole planet, or to just one part of it? Shouldn't we wait and look at some of tomorrow's data before we make a decision? These and other questions were tossed back and forth at the meetings.

No news was announced at the press conferences until most of the questions had been answered, and many of the doubts cleared up. The completely unexpected discovery of the "torus," an invisible donut-shaped circle of charged particles around Jupiter near Io's orbit was the subject of several science meetings. Not until everyone was relatively sure about the composition and nature of this strange region was a report made about it to a press briefing.

THE SCIENCE MEETINGS were the beginning of much more than a series of press releases. No one wanted to hear about the results of the Voyager data more than the scientists themselves. They scribbled notes as they listened to the discussions. Later two or three of them met over lunch in the noisy cafeteria, then over coffee in the afternoon. They argued, compared notes, agreed, expressed their doubts, and shared their enthusiasm. Many times they decided to work together in writing an article for a scientific journal or a popular magazine.

Other articles were written as a result of telephone calls from one part of the country to another. The members of the various investigator teams were located in California's San Fernando Valley and at Harvard University, at Stanford University in California and at Johns Hopkins University in Baltimore. There was constant communication among the people who were members of the same team, and also between the people on different teams. Everyone wanted to share his new discoveries. Everyone was eager to hear about what someone else had just learned.

More papers and articles were written as a result of these conversations. They were read by people all over the world. The authors went to meetings and gave short talks about what they had learned from Voyager 1. The things they wrote about and spoke about sparked ideas in other people's minds. There were more letters and telephone calls that resulted in still more published articles.

At the same time, groups of students, professors, and space scientists were studying and testing the data that had been acquired during the encounter. They wanted to find explanations for the unexpected discoveries that had been made. They were eager to see if the ideas that had sprung from those discoveries were right. They wrote articles telling about their results and comparing the physical makeup of Jupiter to that of Earth.

EVERY IDEA and every scientific result led to another. Some of these ideas and results may be wrong, but the right answer will eventually be found. The twenty-four hours of the Voyager close encounter gave access to a whole new body of knowledge. Long after the spacecraft itself has been lost in space, scientists will still be building on that knowledge. As Ray Bradbury, the famous author, said on March 4, 1979, "Our eyes are traveling through the universe. We are creating new myths, ones based on fact."

[11]

The Super Star
of Space

AS A MEMBER of the Voyager Optical Navigation team, Linda Morabito had spent the month
of February working ten to twelve hours a day,
seven days a week. She had been one of the people responsible for guiding the Voyager 1 spacecraft around
the unknown reefs and shoals of Jupiter and its satellites.

By Friday, March 9, the excitement of the day of
closest approach had begun to dwindle. Linda, along
with the rest of the people on her team, was settling down
to do some more routine work. At 9:30 A.M. she was
peering at a recorded optical navigation picture of Io and
a nearby star. This study was the first step in determining
Voyager 1's exact trajectory through the Jovian region.

At this moment Linda was trying to locate a certain very faint star so she could relate its position in the picture to the position of Io's "limb," or nearest edge.

Linda adjusted her computer to "enhance" the star, or make it stand out more clearly from the background of space. The adjustment happened to include a small section of Io itself. Something about that section caught Linda's attention. On the curve of the horizon there was a fuzzy, umbrella-shaped form. During the past two months Linda had looked at a hundred similar pictures, but she had never seen that irregularity before. Linda wondered if it could be another satellite rising in back of Io.

When she asked the opinion of several other members of her team, they all agreed that the rounded shape couldn't be a moon. None of the known satellites would have been in that position at that particular time, and the object was too big to have remained undiscovered over the years.

Linda took the picture to the neighboring building, so the imaging team could take a look at it. A few of its members processed the photo still further, then asked Ed Stone to study it. More and more people looked at the puzzling feature. As the day passed, the suspicions grew, and the excitement mounted. By 4:30 that afternoon almost everyone was certain that the peculiar object on Io's limb was the plume formed by a volcano. If they were right, it was the first active volcano ever seen outside of Earth! Ray Bradbury had been right when he talked about creating new myths.

Several members of the imaging team worked all through the weekend studying more recorded pictures of Io. A second erupting volcano was found, then another, and another. At least six great explosions were sighted. One of them was spouting material at least 160 miles above Io's surface with the velocity of a high-powered rifle bullet.

"It's the scale of the volcanism that's so staggering," said Brad Smith at a press conference the following week. "If Io were to send a spacecraft to fly past Earth, the chances are slim that it could see even one volcano erupting, and yet Earth is volcanically active. But we go over Io, and things are breaking out all over the place, right under our noses. This discovery is probably the most exciting thing to come out of the Voyager mission so far. It's fantastic!"

Within a few days, pictures of Linda and "her" volcano were spread all over the world. "There it was," wrote one reporter, "puffing like an old wood-burning locomotive."

There it was all right. The mighty Jupiter had been upstaged by one of its moons. Tiny Io was the super star of space.

THE DISCOVERY of the Jovian ring and the Ionian volcanoes left the Voyager project leaders with a big decision to make. March was already half gone. Voyager 2 would be starting its encounter about the middle of May. Based on what had been learned from Voyager 1 before the discovery of the volcanoes, the Voyager 2 sequences had already been changed to study the charged particles of the torus and also the auroras, which are like great rings of glowing lights high in the atmosphere around Jupiter's poles. Time had also been allotted to measure the unexpectedly tremendous amount of lightning in the Jovian atmosphere.

This sequencing still had to have all of the fine details filled in, then it had to be tested by the JPL computers. If everyone worked at a steady pace, the job would be done just in time to uplink the commands for the final encounter phases.

Ray Heacock talked to Charles Stembridge before he made his decision. As the head of the Science Investigation Team, Charles was the one who could tell Ray whether or not there was any chance to reconstruct the sequences to include an intensive study of the volcanoes and the ring. Many of them would have to be done over again, almost from scratch. There was a strong possibility that the work wouldn't be done in time to get them uplinked as they were needed. If the work on the first set was halted, it wouldn't be completed either. In that case, Voyager 2 would be flying with no encounter command loads at all.

Charles talked to many other people about the pros

and cons of doing the volcano watch. The imaging team was strongly in favor of it. Some of the other science teams were against it because they would have to give up many of the measurements they had counted on doing. They wondered why they should give up so much, especially when there was no guarantee that the new sequences would even be completed in time.

There were many calculations and much discussion, before Charles made his decision. He told Ray that his team could do the job. Ray checked with the sequencers and everyone else who would be involved, and made his decision. Voyager 2 was going to have its view of the Ionian volcano country.

Two hundred scientists, mission controllers, sequencers, and engineers went to work on a job that many people still thought was impossible. They had only ten weeks to completely reprogram the fifty-five hours of time around closest approach. This group not only had to devise, design, and change the science commands. It also had to form some sequences that would change some of the engineering commands to a few of the science instruments. Voyager 1 had received a large dose of radiation during its close fly-by of Jupiter. Some of the more sensitive instruments had been endangered. No one wanted that to happen on Voyager 2.

One of the changes was designed to protect the LECP, the Low Energy Charged Particle instrument. It has a detector that originally extended itself beyond a protective shield when it took its measurements. On Voyager 2, Tom Krimigis, the PI for the instrument, decided to switch to a "chicken mode." The programming for the detector was changed so that, instead of coming out all the way, it would just peek around the shielding to make an occasional observation. It wouldn't get as much data that way, but without the chicken mode, the instrument would have to be shut off entirely during the Jupiter encounter. Otherwise, its sensitive detector would be damaged and become useless.

Voyager 2's reprogramming was completed just under the wire. Fourteen hundred memory words had been redone in the sequences, resulting in about a quarter of a million planned encounter events on board the spacecraft. Closest encounter was only three days away when the mission control team began to radio the commands to the spacecraft. Up to that point, this command load was the largest sent at any one time during the Voyager mission.

THE SECOND JUPITER closest encounter held almost as much mystery and sense of anticipation as the first. On Friday, July 6, the spacecraft punched through the bowshock. Fred Scarf's plasma wave instrument recorded a wave of sound that resembled a mighty thunderstorm. "Like David taking on Goliath, the tiny Voyager 2 marched up to the gates of Jupiter," reported the JPL newspaper. "The uplinks and downlinks were never busier."

The spacecraft flicked to within 134,000 miles of Europa and within 40,000 miles of Ganymede. Its cameras took pictures of details that were as small as a mile or two in size. It then tracked Io for the first extraterrestrial volcano watch. For ten hours, from a distance of about 600,000 miles, the cameras took pictures almost every ninety-six seconds. Six volcanoes were in the throes of active eruption. They performed spectacularly, as if on cue.

The volcano watch was everything that anyone could have asked, but old Jupiter had yet another surprise up his sleeve. As Voyager 2 pulled away to start its journey to Saturn, its cameras turned back to look at Jupiter's newly found ring. Just as their shutters clicked, the sun's rays struck the particles in the ring at exactly the right angle. It lit up like a neon sign.

"The fact that the sunlight hit those particles at just the right angle was a lucky accident," said Ray Amorose, the head of the Voyager Flight Control Office. "Linda's discovery of the volcano so soon after encounter was another lucky fluke. If she hadn't enhanced that particular picture to see that faint star more clearly, it might have been several weeks before anyone on the imaging team studied it in depth. Of course, by then it would have been too late for Voyager 2 to have its volcano watch."

* * *

JUST GOOD LUCK? Perhaps. On the other hand, didn't Linda Morabito and many other project people make that good luck happen?

[12]

On to Saturn . . .
and Beyond!

WHILE THE WORLD was still buzzing with the news about the Jupiter encounter, a small group of men and women were working quietly behind the scenes at JPL. At the time that Voyager 1 was swooping beneath Io, they were concentrating on a moon called Titan, and the possibility of finding a primitive form of life upon its surface. As other scientists were gazing with wonder at the Voyager 2 images of the Jovian ring, the minds of these scientists were focused on a still more famous, and far more distant, set of rings.

They were looking ahead to the month of August in 1980 when Voyager 1's cameras would start taking their first high quality pictures of Saturn. The spacecraft was scheduled to have its closest encounter with that planet and six of its moons in November. This group was planning the science measurements that would be taken during that encounter, just as another group had planned the measurements for Jupiter a year and a half earlier.

Again, there were many questions waiting to be answered. How big is the Saturnian magnetic field? How does it interact with the solar wind, the Saturnian rings, and the satellites?

What are those banded structures around Saturn? Is Saturn very similar to Jupiter? Or is it quite different?

Plans were being made to have radio waves trickle through the far side of the rings. It was hoped the rings would be forced to reveal their long-held secrets. Is there a torus around Saturn? Particles that are thrown off from Titan could possibly have formed one. If so, what happens when the solar wind strikes those particles? Do they become charged, as has happened with Io's torus?

What questions should be investigated? Which ones should be left out? This group had many important decisions to make, as had the Jupiter group before them.

The Saturn encounter sequences were being given their final touches in the spring of 1980. Now under the leadership of Nino Lopez, the sequencing team had prepared their blocks of commands based upon the information that was still being gleaned from the Jupiter encounter. They were soon to be uplinked to Voyager 1 and would start to be activated on board the spacecraft on August 22.

The middle of August brought the Voyager team a worry, however. The scan platform began to show evidence of a slow "creep" when it was in a certain position. Since that position was to be used for the first portion of the Saturn encounter, there was good cause for concern.

Fortunately, some quick work by the flight team showed that the problem could be corrected by a slight change in the sequencing.

The team had just begun to relax when another problem arose. It had to do with the star tracker, which is the sensor that locks onto a bright star to control the spacecraft's position. For a while it looked as though it wasn't going to be able to do its job during some important parts of the encounter period. After several days and nights of frantic work, the engineers determined that the tracker could be "pushed" into locking onto the bright stars of Canopus and Vega.

There was a collective sigh of relief from the team members when that news was announced. If any other stars had had to be chosen, the spacecraft would be in a different position relative to Saturn. Most of the important measurements at closest approach would have required new sequencing. There just wasn't enough time to do that much work.

As the spacecraft drew within 64 million miles of Saturn, the mounting excitement could be felt in the air at JPL. One scientist said, "There's a kind of 'before the curtain goes up' feeling. We are really going in and looking at an entirely new place."

The Voyager 1 cameras began to make a Saturn movie by taking a picture every 4.8 minutes for a twenty-four hour period. Pictures of the huge planet began to filter back to Earth and people all over the world were waiting to see them, as they had waited to view the ones from Jupiter.

It soon appeared that, compared to Jupiter, Saturn had a severe case of the "blahs." There were no multi-colored paint splotches, no bright plumes, no white swirling ovals, no Great Red Spots. The planet remained hidden behind a thick blanket of haze, much like the smog that covers some of our large cities.

The pictures may not have been as exciting as could be wished, but the data from the other instruments were beginning to give scientists tantalizing hints about the Saturnian environment. The UV spectrometer "saw" flashes of ultraviolet light near Saturn, and it was evident that there was a large amount of hydrogen gas around the planet out to and beyond the orbit of its largest moon, Titan.

November 12 was to be the day of closest approach. As it drew near, the eyes of the scientific world were again focused upon the Jet Propulsion Laboratory. Every morning reporters, television crews, and writers clamored for admission to the grounds.

"The sense of adventure is unparalleled," said Carl Sagan. "We are at the moment of extraordinary discovery."

Everyone who was present for the upcoming events shared his anticipation. Early in November, Voyager sent down images that showed some of Saturn's lower altitude clouds and its banded atmosphere. It was found that the planet's equator is swept by winds traveling as fast as 900 miles an hour. Saturn appeared to be like Jupiter in many ways, and yet in other ways it seemed mysteriously different. For instance, all of its bands appeared to be going in one direction instead of the eddies and whorls of Jupiter's rings.

On November 11, Voyager 1 punched through Saturn's bowshock, and close approach began. The spacecraft soared past the moon, Titan, and from a distance of only 2500 miles "sniffed" at its atmosphere. The next day, it gathered speed and rushed toward, then under, the plane of Saturn's rings. Next, it flew past five more moons and the planet itself. On Thursday it took backward glances at Saturn and flew past still another moon.

Throughout the encounter, the downlinked data presented wondrous surprises to the waiting Voyager team and to the world. The spacecraft's performance proved to be the equal of the marvels its instruments were discovering. Voyager 1's peak velocity reached 56,600 miles per hour, and it skirted within 77,200 miles of Saturn's cloud tops. So precisely did it follow its commands that at no time was it more than 46 seconds off schedule or more than 12 miles off course.

The slightly battered and worn Voyager 1 still has one more job to do before it disappears into interstellar space. During the next few years, its instruments will measure the flow of solar particles to determine where the sun's influence ends and that of the stars begins. This "heliopause" marks the outer boundary of our solar system.

ALL THROUGH the days and nights preceding, during, and after the closest planetary approach, the Voyager science teams were sorting through the flood of data they were receiving. Within one week, they had learned more about the Saturnian system than had been learned in all the centuries up to that point. Three new Saturnian moons were discovered. The known moons took on new and unique identities and became visible places instead of just ancient names. There were fractured moons, pitted moons, and moons that were cratered almost to the point of distinction. One of them, Mimas, had an impact crater that covered almost a fourth of its entire surface. In contrast, Enceladus presented an almost smooth surface. Why? Perhaps Voyager 2 will answer that question.

Two very small satellites orbited close to Saturn's outermost ring. They appeared to be acting, as one reporter said, "like dogs herding sheep along a narrow road, the outer moon seems to be keeping ring particles from flying off into space, while the inner moon stops them from falling toward Saturn."

It was suggested that they be named Lassie 1 and Lassie 2 in keeping with their doglike activities.

Two other small moons were about fifty miles in diameter, and they orbited within thirty miles of each other. Each time they drew near to each other, a collision seemed inevitable, but at the last minute one of them would speed up and the other would slow down. They had evidently been playing this game of "cosmic chicken" with each other for eons.

Titan was dethroned as the largest satellite in our solar system when it was found to be slightly smaller than Ganymede. The Saturnian moon was found to be unique in another, more special, way, however. It's the only known satellite to have a dense nitrogen gas atmosphere.

The Saturnian moons were fascinating, but it was the planet's ring system that drove Brad Smith to say, "We thought we had seen all there was to see, but in the strange world of Saturn's rings, the bizarre has become commonplace."

Most of the Voyager's scientists agreed with him. It

had been thought that the system consisted of six large rings. From the planet outward, they were called D, C, B, A, F, and E, having been named in the order of discovery. The prying eyes of the Voyager cameras revealed that these six rings are actually hundreds of little ringlets that are made of icy particles. Each of the ringlets circles Saturn within its own orbit. The entire system resembles a giant phonograph record that is 670,000 miles in diameter.

It was discovered that the Cassini division, which had appeared to be an empty gap between the A and B rings, contained several of the ringlets.

The pictures of the B ring produced another startling surprise. It was seen to contain dark bands that form and reform as the ring rotates around the planet. The bands were compared to the spokes of a bicycle wheel. The appearance of these spokes bewildered the Voyager scientists. How do those particles remain in place? they wondered. According to the laws of physics, the particles on the outside of an orbiting ring move slower than the particles on the inside of that ring. As a result the spokes should be pulled apart almost immediately and the particles permanently distributed throughout the ring. Their appearance is a puzzle that remains to be solved.

The F ring revealed its own special secret. It was seen to consist of two separate rings that crisscross each other in a loosely braided fashion. Like the spokes, the braided rings seem to be defying the laws of orbital mechanics.

EVEN BEFORE the Voyager 1's Saturn encounter was over, a group of men and women were at work designing the encounter sequences for Voyager 2's Saturn encounter. They now had an entire new body of knowledge upon which to base those sequences. At the final press conference some of the amazing facts were summed up.

"We've all had a great ride in the last twelve days," concluded Ed Stone. "It's been so smooth that it's easy to forget that it took eight or nine years to get the spacecraft there. It took thousands of people to build it, and flying it took the combined efforts of all of us here at JPL and the crews at the DSN stations.

"We've been caught up in the rush of discovery, and now we have to find out exactly what it is we've learned. We have enough puzzles to keep us busy for many, many years."

People in Japan, Europe, Canada, Mexico, and South America had seen that rush of discovery on their television sets. So had Rusty Schwickart, the astronaut. He compared the Voyager mission with the explorations of Sir Francis Drake and Columbus. "But there's one important difference," he said. "The whole world has been able to share the sense of mystery and discovery of the two Voyagers. The new worlds in space are open to everyone here on Earth."

Nine months after the Voyager 1 Saturn encounter, Voyager 2 was scheduled to arrive at that planet. It was to take a different path than that of its sister ship, because it would have to use Saturn's gravity assist to start its journey to Uranus. The Saturn-Uranus cruise will take four years. When Voyager 2 finally reaches that distant planet, it will sail past the satellite, Miranda, then pass behind Uranus so its instruments can look back upon the planet's southern hemisphere and its south pole. After testing, measuring, and probing the atmosphere, the spacecraft will begin its flight to Neptune.

When the Neptune encounter is over, the Voyager odyssey will at last be completed.

[13]

An Endless Journey

WHEN ITS final investigation is done, Voyager 2 will join Voyager 1 in its journey through the vastness of space. Like two aging explorers with no goal and no home, they will sail on forever. During the 21st century, they will wend their way through the eerie realm that forms the far reaches of our solar system. Eventually, they will break free from our Sun's gravitational pull and head toward the constellation Capricorn.

By this time the gravitational pull of the Sun will have slowed them down to a speed of only ten kilometers a second. One hundred thousand years will pass before either one approaches a star. Space is so enormous and so empty that it will be another million years before they approach another one. Perhaps it will be a blinding blue-white ball, or a giant red puff of a cool-burning star, or a small, white hot very dense body. Occasionally, one of the Voyagers may pass near the cold, black, burned-out corpse of an ancient star.

Even if there is some sort of civilization in interstellar space, it's unlikely that either Voyager will ever find it. However, if one of them does, and if those beings can navigate in space, the spacecraft will arouse their curiosity. What is this strange, scarred relic that has drifted, uninvited, into our realm? they will wonder.

Cautiously at first, then with mounting excitement, they will examine the Voyager. During this examination, they will find the souvenirs of Earth that its makers placed aboard it so many long eons ago.

These beings will pore over the photographs, diagrams, and drawings that represent life as it existed on the planet Earth. Will they find any meaning in them? Perhaps not, because our bodily forms and all the things that are familiar to us will be totally alien to this future civilization.

The discoverers of Voyager will no doubt puzzle over the first cosmic LP, a two hour phonograph record that was put together under the direction of astronomer Carl Sagan. What will they think when they hear the greetings from Earth spoken in fifty-three languages? Will they respond to the musical selections? And which will they prefer—Bach or Chuck Berry?

They'll listen to the roar of our surf, the soft thump of a human heartbeat, and the cry of a baby. They'll hear the sounds of our animal life—the chirping of birds and crickets, the trumpeting of elephants, and the ethereal, melodic songs of a whale.

Will they understand the words of President Jimmy Carter? "This is a present from a small distant world, a token of our sounds, our images, our thoughts, and our feelings. . . . This record represents our hopes and our determination, and our good will in a vast and awesome universe."

Perhaps this golden disk will be heard some millions of years in the future. Let's hope that it will be understood. If it is, the thousands of people who made the Voyager space mission possible will have made their ultimate contribution to every human being who ever existed on Earth. They will have tied all of us into an unending chain of universal life.

THE VOYAGER MISSION
INVESTIGATIONS

Infrared Interferometer Spectrometer and Radiometer (IRIS) The IRIS instrument is used to gather information about the temperatures and the composition of the atmospheres or surfaces of the planets and their satellites. It measures the heat that the planets radiate at infrared frequencies. It was also designed to collect data about the composition, distribution, and size of the particles of matter within Saturn's rings.

PRINCIPAL INVESTIGATOR: RUDOLF HANEL

Photopolarimeter This instrument was designed to measure the intensity of scattered light at certain optical frequencies. It provides information about the physical and chemical composition of particles of matter in the atmospheres of planets and satellites. It's also used to obtain data on the satellites' surfaces.

PRINCIPAL INVESTIGATOR: CHARLES LILLIE

Ultraviolet Spectrometer The UV spectrometer is used to study the thermal structure of the planets' upper atmospheres, and also to measure helium and hydrogen densities in interplanetary and interstellar space. The data from this instrument led to the discovery of the torus near Io's orbit.

PRINCIPAL INVESTIGATOR: A. LYLE BROADFOOT

Radio Science The Voyager radio equipment is used basically for communication, but it was also designed to provide scientific information. The signals give information about the size of the planets and their satellites, their atmospheres and the composition of rings. At selected points along the encounter trajectories, the planets are located between the spacecraft and Earth. At these times of "occultation" the radio waves pass through the planetary atmospheres. By studying those waves, scientists can learn much about the structure and conditions that exist in those atmospheres.

PRINCIPAL INVESTIGATOR: VON R. ESHLEMAN

Cosmic Rays Cosmic rays are particles that travel through space at speeds nearly equal to that of light. They often come into the solar system from elsewhere in the galaxy. This instrument gathers data on the electrical charge, mass, and energy of those particles. It also measures the variation in their number at different times, places, and arrival directions.

PRINCIPAL INVESTIGATOR: R. E. VOGT

Low-Energy Charged Particles (LECP) This instrument deals with particles that contain lower energy than do cosmic rays. It gathers data during both the planetary encounters and in interplanetary space.
PRINCIPAL INVESTIGATOR: S. M. KRIMIGIS

Plasma Particles The solar wind is not a smoothly flowing current. Its speed fluctuates greatly at certain times, for instance when it runs into a planet's magnetosphere. This instrument furnishes information about the solar wind's interaction with the magnetosphere and about the composition of the solar wind, and conditions inside a magnetosphere.
PRINCIPAL INVESTIGATOR: HERBERT BRIDGE

Magnetic Fields The spacecraft's magnetometer investigates the magnetic fields of the planets, and the sun, and also the interactions of the satellites with the planetary magnetospheres.
PRINCIPAL INVESTIGATOR: NORMAN NESS

Plasma Waves This instrument investigates the dynamics of the planetary magnetospheres. It gathers data on the interactions between charged plasma particles and plasma waves, and on lightning in the planetary atmospheres.
PRINCIPAL INVESTIGATOR: FREDERICK L. SCARF

Planetary Radio Astronomy During the cruise phases and planetary encounters, this instrument measures the radio emissions of the planets. When combined with other information, these data help to determine the origin of those emissions. The investigation also helps to show the relationship of a planet's radio emissions to its satellites.

PRINCIPAL INVESTIGATOR: JAMES WARWICK

Imaging Science Wide angle and narrow angle cameras take pictures of the cloud layers surrounding the planets and also of the satellite surfaces. From these pictures scientists learn about the motion, structure, and colors of the various cloud belts, and also about the geological makeup of the satellite surfaces.

PRINCIPAL INVESTIGATOR: BRADFORD SMITH

GLOSSARY

AACS Attitude and Articulation Control Subsystem. A computer that keeps the spacecraft stable and on course. It also moves the scan platform into position.

Amalthea Innermost of the larger Jovian satellites.

Announcement of Flight Opportunity A bulletin distributed by NASA to give scientists and engineers news of a proposed mission.

Asteroid One of thousands of very small planets that orbit the sun between the orbits of Mars and Jupiter.

Bit A brief pulse emitted by the radio communications system of the spacecraft. These signal pulses represent the letter or numbers that make up the messages.

Bowshock An invisible boundary where the solar wind meets the outer edge of a planet's magnetic field.

Burn A firing of a set of spacecraft thrusters.

Canopus A very bright star that is used as a reference point, along with the Earth and the Sun, to keep the spacecraft stable.

CCS Command Control Subsystem. This computer is the

"brains" of the spacecraft. It stores commands, then at the correct time relays them to the other two on-board computers.

Callisto One of Jupiter's large satellites.

Centaur The second stage liquid propellant rocket of the Voyager launch vehicle.

Charged particle A particle of matter that has become charged with electricity.

Command load A block, or set, of commands that are designed to guide the spacecraft and to direct the investigations during a certain time period.

Cruise The time spent by the spacecraft traveling from Earth to a planet encounter, or from one encounter to the next.

Downlink The process of sending radio signals from the spacecraft to Earth.

DSN Deep Space Network. The worldwide chain of tracking stations that enable man to maintain constant communication with the spacecraft during its flight.

Encounter The closest approach of a spacecraft to a planet or satellite.

Europa One of Jupiter's large satellites.

FDS Flight Data Subsystem. This computer collects and dispatches the scientific and engineering data that has been collected by the instruments on board the spacecraft.

Frequency The number of times a process is repeated during a certain period of time. The Voyager spacecraft radio transmission frequencies are much lower than visible light frequencies.

Ganymede One of Jupiter's large satellites.

Gravity assist The billiard ball effect that occurs when a planet's gravitational pull causes the spacecraft to speed up, be deflected, then hurled on toward the next planet.

Hydrazine A liquid chemical fuel on board the spacecraft that is converted to a gas in a thruster for attitude control.

Imaging system The spacecraft's camera system.

Io One of Jupiter's large moons.

IRIS Infrared interferometer spectrometer and radiometer. One of the instruments on the spacecraft.

JPL Jet Propulsion Laboratory.

Launch window The time during which a spacecraft must be launched if it is to reach its target.

Magnetosphere The region of space around a planet within which that planet's magnetic field is dominant.

MDS Mission Design Team. The group of specialists

that is responsible for the prelaunch planning of a space mission.

Meteoroid A piece of solid matter floating in space.

Mission Control Team The real time monitors of the spacecraft.

Mission Operations Team The group that is responsible for the day-to-day operation of the spacecraft.

Mission Planning Office At launch time, the MDS becomes the Mission Planning Office. Its members must make the long-range flight plans and be aware of possible problems.

Mission profile. The itinerary of the flight of the spacecraft. It's divided into various phases into which are fitted the scientific and engineering events.

MJS77 Mariner-Jupiter-Saturn, 1977. The prelaunch title of the Voyager mission.

Non-real time (1) A spacecraft command that is not to be immediately put into effect. (2) An analysis of data that's done hours, days, or weeks after these data were received.

Optical navigation The process of pinpointing the location of the spacecraft by relating its position to planets and known stars.

Pioneer 10 and 11 Two spacecraft that were launched in 1972. They scouted ahead to the outer planets and sent back data that were helpful to the Voyager mission planners.

Plasma An ionized gas. It differs from ordinary gas in that it's a good conductor of electricity and is affected by a magnetic field.

Plasma waves Movements within clouds of ionized gas.

Radiation The process of emitting energy in the form of waves.

Radiant energy Energy that travels in a wavelike motion, such as radio or light waves.

Real time (1) A command that is to be acted upon immediately. (2) The monitoring of the spacecraft data as they come into the Space Flight Operations Center.

RTG Radioisotope thermoelectric generator. A nuclear fuel device used to power the spacecraft by changing heat into electricity.

S-band frequency The low-rate frequency that is used to transmit ordinary engineering information plus the scientific information that is sent back during the cruise phases.

Satellite A body in space that orbits another body of a larger size. A moon.

Sequence A succession of commands transmitted to the spacecraft.

Solar wind A stream of electrically charged particles emitted from the sun.

Space Flight Operations Center The hub of the mission. It's here that the communication between Earth and the spacecraft begins and ends.

Spectrometer A device that analyzes light from a gas in order to determine the composition of that gas.

Titan (1) Saturn's largest satellite. (2) The first-stage solid propellant rocket of the Voyager launch vehicle.

Trajectory A flight path.

Torus An invisible donut-shaped cloud of charged particles.

Uplink The process of sending commands up to the spacecraft.

Venus mission A space mission during which the planet Venus and its atmosphere was explored.

Viking mission A mission during which Mars was orbited and two vehicles were landed upon its surface.

X-band frequency The very high frequency that's used by the spacecraft transmitter during encounters for high-data-rate science return.

INDEX